The Au

Linda M Noon

THE AWAKENING OF THE LOTUS

A Personal Story Of My Awakening To My Truth In The Times Of The 21st Century And The Covid-19 Pandemic.
LOTUS Light of the Universal Source.

By

Linda Michelle Noon

Linda M Noon

The Awakening of the Lotus

First Print Edition

October 2020

First published in USA 2020

978-0-9874621-1-4

Cover Image by: Myecovermaker.com

Linda M Noon

This book is dedicated to:

All who are awake, awakening or just curious.

To my family and friends, awake or still sleeping, believers or non-believers. Those who I know I drove nuts by talking about what I felt and believed, for listening to me, especially Sheila Warne.

For my Grandchildren, in the hope they get to know me and remember me for being who I am. Although many think I am nuts, I don't feel I am.

A thank you to Ted Exley, a friend from the 1980s who I once worked with, for inspiring me to write after I told him "I might write a book". I told him I did not know what to write about, he replied "being awake". Ted is also awake.

Linda M Noon

Table of Contents

Introduction...1

PART I: SLEEPING IN THE MUD 5

    Chapter One: While I Was Sleeping 7

    Chapter Two: The Knowing 19

    Chapter Three: Fine Tuning 37

    Chapter Four: It Gets Better................................45

    Chapter Five: The Dark Night Of The Soul..........63

    Chapter Six: Merging Lotus........................ 71

PART II: Covid-19...89

    Chapter Seven: 2019-2020...................91

    Chapter Eight: The Death Of George Floyd........103

    Chapter Nine: The Australian Narrative...........109

    Chapter Ten: The Deep State & Cabal............119

    Chapter Eleven: Freedom Day........................129

Epilogue/Conclusion...141

Bibliography 143

Acknowledgments...145

About the Author 147

Linda M Noon

Introduction

The topic of this book is about how I have awakened over the years psychically, spiritually and everything in between, but my inspiration has been the year of 2020 with the great Pandemic Covid-19. By finding and connecting with like-minded friends and people from all around the world through Facebook, meditation, spiritual growth classes, road trips and meeting interesting people along the way.

The contents of this book are my stories and experiences, but most of all it is my truth. Finally, I feel like I can speak through these pages without judgement. Some may share the same truth or resonate with what I am writing about, and some may not. I would like to share my truth in the hope it may help many others, in their search for their own truth, to help awaken you to what innate, dormant gifts you possess, to uplift you on your path in life.

My goal is for my story to help many who feel isolated, alone, scared or may have experienced similar things to me, but at times felt you were slightly mad. Unable to talk and share with others your experiences, feelings, and thoughts.

I am by no means an expert, scientist or doctor and nor do I wish to be. From what I have researched and discovered, most know as little as I do, simply because with everything I have read there have been contradictions and their information changes to suit the narrative of what is going on in the world right now. I wish not to convert you into becoming a Donald Trump supporter either; it is not about who you choose to support, I only hope that you may keep an open mind if you choose to go down the 'Rabbit hole'.

I am neither left-wing nor right-wing, I actually do not understand why one is labelled one or the other, because I follow what resonates within me, and that could be a mixture of them both. I do not know all of the policies and beliefs of either side. There is a saying: the left-wing and the right-wing are of the same bird. Just like my left arm and my right arm are of the same human.

I do, however, hold a Diploma Certificate as a Qualified Clinical Hypnotherapist since 2002. I have been practicing on and off since that time, as well as many other certificates. I have studied many things of interest to me, to improve and upskill for one reason or another, whether it be to improve my employment chances or just wanting to learn.

I have worked as a cleaner at a hospital, and as an aircraft cleaner at Manchester airport in the UK, a job I enjoyed. I worked as a kitchen hand, on Tarot telephone lines, as well as working for the Government as a Public Servant for many years. I have also been self-employed in a Healing Centre which offered meditation classes, spiritual workshops, Reiki classes, Tarot readings and Hypnotherapy.

I spent three years studying and learning about the nature of the Mind and the Philosophy of Buddhism and Buddhist meditation with a Senior Abbot Buddhist Monk from Vietnam, Venerable Master Thang, as well as being a member of his committee at his Temple. That was a very blessed time in my life. Now I'm unemployed because, just when I was getting my Hypnotherapy and website up and running again, Covid-19 struck the world, the restrictions and lockdowns do not allow me to see clients, hence more inspiration to write this book.

I am hopeful the words I have written within these pages serve to empower my audience to create something out of this dark, uncertain time. Maybe that is to become more creative in a craft or art or something you can do from home because I can't see this virus going away anytime soon.

The information I am writing about has helped me see things in a very different light. I feel awake, and I believe the more people who awaken, the better our chances as a humane, compassionate race will be to succeed in creating a free, liberated, beautiful world post Covid-19.

Not only for us but for our children, grandchildren, and their future. I believe the planet needs more awakened ones to help raise the vibration, so we, as a whole collective consciousness will achieve and create a much better world than the one we live in at this present time.

I hope to gently remind you not to extend your problems but to act upon them, to find solutions to enrich your life and the lives of those around you. The earlier you awaken to truth, the better the world will become, purely born from the act of love instead of fear. I have lived in fear for far too long, and I know only too well of the unpleasantness it brings. We see all around us right now the mass collective fear that every single being is experiencing. I wish to write this book the way I speak but also coming from a space of love, not intellect. If the information contained within these pages awakens only one person, then that is one more than before, and it will have been successful.

I endeavour to attain my truth in the knowledge of that which I have experienced and felt throughout my life, even if I do not understand it. There is a certain amount of inner peace which occurs in acceptance, which allows you to move on, until the next inexplicable experience arrives.

Linda M Noon

PART I: SLEEPING IN THE MUD

Where We All Begin After Birth

The title above SLEEPING IN THE MUD is my metaphor for being unaware. It is not anyone's fault because this is how our conditioning begins. A conditioning that has been passed down from generation to generation and with the enormous help of television and social media. The aim of this book is to awaken the Lotus within us all.

From birth we are conditioned to be how our parents are, the world around us, siblings, aunties, uncles, cousins, friends and even pets. As we grow, we do not know any difference nor are we fully aware of the outside world. We experience no fear because we solely rely on our parents to feed us, love us, and protect us. We are totally reliant on them for everything. We do not know if we are rich or poor, boy or girl, and we have no concept of whether we are safe or in any danger. We do not know what part of the world we live in and we are exceptionally vulnerable beings, but a mother's instinct is to love and protect their baby, child, and children. Don't get me wrong, not all mothers do, but the majority do.

There is no concept of those daily basic needs other then we know when we are hungry, cold, warm or in pain. Then the whole household knows all about it. I often wonder what a baby may think or even if a baby does think, especially when a newborn looks at you. Sometimes there is a feeling that the newborn is looking straight into your soul in a dazed and confused manner wondering where the heck they are or even who the heck are you looking back at them.

Over time a baby's awareness begins to develop; they begin to smile and recognise you and those around them. Their eyes become brighter as though they are now fully present in their world and surroundings. They begin to respond to your voice, sounds, touch, tastes and smells. All of these things happen over time naturally in the sequence of their development and the activity going on in the brain.

There is great excitement with the first smile, the first words, their every movement in their growth, crawling, walking, talking and their beautiful hugs, kisses, and giggles. It is an amazing time for both the child and the parents. Your baby loves you so much, and although still very reliant upon you, they begin to develop an individual personality, but the best part is that your child is not prejudiced, your child is not full of anger, fear or conditioning. This, I believe, is why when you become an adult a part of you longs to be a child once again. As you look back upon your childhood you remember the freedom of good times not having any worries about life at all. That is unless something traumatic happened to you in your early years.

I believe that even a small child knows when it has been abused in some form whether it is physically, mentally or emotionally because they feel it in their soul. They may not understand it logically or intellectually because it is a feeling, a deep inner knowing without mentally recalling the incident or incidents. Your soul just knows because it happened on a very deep spiritual level.

As we grow and mature into a teenager or adult most of us have actually looked back on our lives growing up and recalled a time when something happened knowing it was not right and only as a grown-up you realised, "Hey that was not right, but we just thought it was normal." Only when you experience the outside world do you realise that *your* world was very small, restricted and limited. By which time you are also conditioned through your family, schools, media, friends, words and experiences that what you have been through was either good or bad.

Chapter One: While I Was Sleeping

*Just Like The Lotus We Too Have The Ability
To Rise From The Mud.*

I was born Linda Michelle Noon in 1962 in a place in northern England called Salford.

Salford was not a pretty place, it was adorned in poverty, but it was a very happy place. Some of my friends here in Australia always thought I was saying "Soul Food" when asked where I was born. I have three siblings and I was the third child born.

We lived in a three-story, old Victorian house, the third floor was an attic and a creepy one at that. We had no bathroom and outside toilet and a cellar full of coal for the open fire. In the cellar was an old tin bath that made a weekly appearance for us kids to have our weekly bath, every day was usually a wash in the sink or a rough flannel scrapped across our skin. Describing this house now in 2020 sounds like I was in a scene from 'Oliver'.

We had no garden only cobbled streets with a grid at every front door that the Coalman would lift to deliver our weekly coal supply down into the cellar. All of the houses were attached like a scene out of Coronation Street and the street lights were old gas lights converted to electric. There was also a back entry and a small paved yard (what we called Flags).

The second floor consisted of only two bedrooms for six people. I had to share a double bed with my two older brothers, them at the top and me at the bottom in between their feet. I did not have a pillow so I learnt to sleep on my folded arm. My baby sister slept in my parents' room.

So, bleak as it may sound, those were some of the best years of my life. Everyone knew everyone. Kids played on the streets from morning until night. It was not odd for people to visit for a cuppa and to borrow a cup of sugar and everyone was the 'salt of the earth'. I am still in contact with some of the neighbours to this day.

We lived in Salford until I was seven years old. The point here is, I did not know anything different other than my family, friends and my school. I had no conception of poverty, fear or anything of the likes. I didn't really think any other world existed except the one I was in. I loved it, especially when we had a street party. All the ladies would bring out their kitchen table and join them all in a row in the street. Each household would make something to share for the kids such as jelly, fairy bread, cupcakes and jugs of cordial. Oh, and jam butties, which was just jam on bread.

I also remember that my dad was the only person ever to own a car or a Triumph motorbike and sidecar, every opportunity he got away from work, he would take us camping somewhere. Dad was brought up on a farm during the Second World War, being an only child, that is where they sent the boys back then, so he had a great love of farms, camping and outdoors. Devon and Cornwall were the places our dad would take us. He also once took us on the ferry across to Ireland, I remember a place called Cork. Most times he would just wing it, pack the car with us lot and off we'd go with his tent. It was absolutely marvellous!

My dad was a long-distance lorry driver after he finished his time in the Army, then he joined the Territorial Army, he loved driving. My mum was a machinist making eiderdowns and often worked at home with a large industrial machine that was operated with a foot peddle. Sometimes with the scraps of material left she would make my sister and me a dress or two because usually, our clothes were from the opportunity shops.

My grandmother and grandfather on my mother's side were my guardian angels, and I had a very special bond with them both. I was their pet and I often spent a weekend or a week with them in another area called Wythenshawe. I loved going there because I got my own bed and great meals of homemade stews, I even got to have a proper bath. I did not know my grandparents on my dad's side because my dad's dad died when he was nine, and his mother died when I was one.

Up to around the age of five I had a lovely life, laughing with friends every day, feeling the love of my grandparents, everything was so good. Not a worry in the world, I never felt any emotional pain, even though looking back now at certain situations there must have been some, but at the time I did not know any different.

My first encounter with emotional pain was when my grandfather passed away. I was five years old and it was right on Christmas. When he was in Wythenshawe Hospital, he asked my dad to bring me for a visit and this was at a time when children were not allowed inside an Adult Ward. Fortunately for me, my grandad was on the ground floor. The last time I saw him was when my dad took me to the hospital and put me on his shoulders to wave at grandad through the window. Grandad was wearing striped blue and white pyjamas, and we were both waving like mad at one another through the window. That memory still brings a tear to my eyes.

That was the last time I ever saw him, and back in those days, children were not even allowed to go to funerals. I remember being absolutely gutted when he died, the pain I felt then as a five-year-old is still with me today, that was the first time I felt a broken heart, I cried and cried and cried.

A week later was Christmas day and I remember watching some old black and white movie about a dog that got lost and the owner could not find it. I felt a lump in my throat and I cried and cried, but the tears were for my grandad. My mum appeared in the doorway and she said, "What are you crying at?" I replied, "I want my grandad." Mum said in a shout, "Don't you be crying because you will make me cry." So I tried to hold it in, the pain in my throat when I did that was excruciating.

That day I learnt to keep my sad feelings to myself because I did not want to upset anyone else. Fortunately, I still had my gran who asked for me to visit even more after grandad died. I went gladly to be with her, it was lovely. I spent lots of time with her, and she used to call me her little piece of toast because apparently, I kept her warm in bed, better than a hot water bottle.

My world slowly returned to normal and life went on. I soon became a happy child again, although I was quiet and shy mainly at home, it was a different story outside. I had lots of friends. My first best friend was Margaret Veevers, we got on so well, and I still have contact with her today, mainly through Facebook, but I did see her in 2012.

Now, I don't want this book to be a morbid tale as that is not what I am trying to achieve here, I am trying to make others aware how I woke up and how life and events helped to mould me into a fearful person through experiences and conditioning.

Fast forward a few months, still in Salford, still living a life in sleep mode. I used to go to school with a girl called Susan Buckley, who lived around the corner. Each day we walked to school together and played in the yard together. One day a man appeared at the railings that surrounded our school, Stawells Memorial Primary School. When I say man, he could have been anything between sixteen to early twenties, to us that was a man.

He engaged us in conversation every day and we thought he was really nice. Every day he appeared at the railings, and for maybe a week or two he spoke to us and we spoke to him. One day he asked us if we would like to go to the park after school and we said 'yes' with great excitement. We arranged to meet him after school as back in those days we walked to and from school on our own, no parents to hold our hands.

The last bell sounded out as school came to an end for the day, quickly we ran to meet this man and there he was at the railings, we were so excited to be going to a park, so off we went. I don't recall the name of the park, but I do remember it was also surrounded by railings, with beautiful flower beds, and lush green lawns, so in our eyes it was very posh. It did not feel like it was far away from where we lived. I remember we were playing in some shrubbed area which was still nice, but I do not remember playing on swings or slides.

Suddenly this man asked us to come into the bush area and said we were playing a game. Although I do not remember the context of the game, I do know it was not sexual. The man said that I should pretend that he had killed me and buried me in a shallow grave and there in the shrub was a shallow grave which I lay down in while he covered me with leaves. How trippy!

After a while I began to notice that it was getting dusk and I saw another man locking the gates of the park in the distance, it was only then that I began to cry that I wanted to go home. To which the man said, "Okay, I will pass you over the railings," which he did, but we still arranged to meet again on another day.

After he passed us over the railings, we quickly walked home in case it got dark, I knew I was going to be in trouble when I arrived home for not coming straight home from school. As Susan and I walked down towards our street, I saw my dad's blue van coming flying towards us like a bat out of hell. Out he jumped and demanded we both get into the van.

Dad then drove us straight to the local Police station, where we were greeted by a Bobby who took us inside to his office and gave us the biggest telling-off of our lives. He even put us inside a cell and said, "If you ever do not come home from school again, you will be locked up in there with only bread and water to eat." We cried with sheer terror, mainly because we did not think what we had done was so wrong.

11

We never saw the man who talked us into going to the park again, so I am not sure what happened to him, we did tell the Bobby he was coming back again to get us. Maybe he was arrested, I don't know. More scary though, it was around the times of Ian Brady and Myra Hindley. If you don't know who they are, Google them.

I can see as I write how I was beginning to become aware of the world around me. I was developing fear and conditioning because of actions I had taken. I was naïve, vulnerable and innocent. I needed to have a sense of danger about me, or I could have been murdered, but I only became scared when the park gates were locked and it was getting dark. Susan and I were very, very lucky!

When I was around seven years old, we moved to another area of the UK, a place called Lemmington Spa in Warwickshire. My dad's uncle had become sick and we had to move to live with him as Dad became his carer. That meant we gave up the Council house in Salford to go live in what I describe as a 'posh place'. I missed my friends from Salford as they were the only people I had ever known.

I was bullied by my class teacher at that new school, and she made me feel like a commoner. It was there that I began to feel isolated and not good enough. I never liked Lemmington Spa, although there were lovely country lanes not far from where we lived that we could ride to on a bike, we had a garden, a bathroom and I had my own little box room bedroom for the first time.

After eighteen months a situation arose between my parents and the uncle, we could not go back to Salford, although I hoped we could. We had nowhere to go, we had given up the Council house in Salford. So my dad said we were going to live in Australia, this was 1971, and we were going on a ship. I was excited about that although I knew nothing about Australia. I was happy to get out of Lemmington Spa. I was eight years old, almost nine.

I loved being on the ship, the Fair Sky, six weeks of it, except for the storms we sailed through that tossed us all over the place. One night the storm was so bad that every passenger had to sit in the Lounge/Ballroom area. I was sat at a large round table with my family and dad's new friends that we met on the ship, and we were all playing cards. I was on a chair when the ship tilted to one side, I began to slide across the dance floor and the pull and gravity kept me on the chair. Everyone was yelling, "Jump! Jump!" but I couldn't. Then from nowhere I got the courage to jump, and I rolled under a couch that was bolted to the floor and got wedged there but happy to say I did not get hurt. Some people had been tossed out their beds and sustained broken arms in some of those storms.

There was a cabin steward that used to do the rounds; he was Italian, mid-twenties maybe, quite handsome, I guess. He used to pass us every day and smile and say hello. One night there was a fancy-dress party for adults and children over age ten, that meant my sister and I were not permitted to go. The theme was Pirates. Dad and his new friend Tony were done up like Pirates, painted on beards and scarves on their heads, shirtless. My older brother Mick had drawn tattoos on them both with black charcoal. Mick was a great artist.

My sister Tracey and I were locked inside the cabin we shared with Mum, there was a single bed and a bunk bed. I slept on the single bed near the porthole. Mum had gone to the party with Dad and the boys. My sister and I were locked inside the cabin and we could not get out.

A short time later as my sister and I were lying in our beds talking to each other, we heard a key in the door, thinking they were back already. When the door opened it was the Steward; he said he had come to tuck us in. We thought, "How nice." The Steward tucked my sister in and gave her a kiss on the cheek, then he tucked me in and gave me a kiss on the mouth. I thought, "Why did he do that to me?" But I passed it off as no big deal. Soon my sister and I fell asleep, locked inside our cabin.

Sometime later, how much later I do not know, I began to wake up to a presence in the room. I woke up and there sat on my bed right next to me was the Steward. He had taken the blankets off me, my nightdress was up around my neck, exposing my torso. As I gave out a blood-curdling scream, my sister woke up and screamed too just because I was screaming. The Steward tried to keep me quiet by saying, "Shush! Shush!" with his finger at his mouth. I did not stop screaming and began to cry. The Steward then ran out of the cabin, locking us back inside.

I was hysterical, suddenly the door opened up again, only this time it was my brother Steve who was older than us. Mum had sent him to check on us. When he saw the state I was in, and I told him there was a man in our cabin, he ran off to fetch Mum and Dad. It was not much longer when almost half of the ship arrived at the cabin door, Mum, Dad and a Ship Counsellor with a crowd behind them. As I was describing to the Counsellor what had taken place, she turned to my parents and said, "This was not a dream."

At that point my dad, Tony and an entourage of people went looking for this Steward, the funny part was they were all dressed up like Pirates still, it was like 'Mutiny on the Bounty'. Thankfully they did not find him. I reckon my dad and Tony would have killed him and thrown him overboard. We were told I was going to the Captain's Office in the morning and every Steward who worked on the ship would appear one by one in the door threshold, and I was to point him out when he appeared.

The next morning we sat patiently waiting to go to the Captain's Office I was sitting on Dad's knee, terrified but feeling safe because my dad was there, and so was Mum. Finally, we were called to the Captain's Office. I was still on Dad's knee when one by one, the Stewards appeared in the doorway. It seemed to go on forever as one by one they passed but not the Steward that had entered the cabin. Eventually, he appeared and I yelled, "That's him." As I did so, Dad leapt up and made a mad dash for him and I landed on my feet as I fell from Dad's knee. The other Stewards had managed to shield the Steward from my dad's fist as they locked the door closed.

The Captain told us that the Steward would be locked up until we reached the next Port and the next one was South Africa, there he would be removed and arrested. Until we reached the next Port, I did not feel safe even though I never saw the Steward.

When we arrived in South Africa all the passengers were allowed to disembark for a day trip around the town, as we were walking around the town Dad and Tony were ahead of us, I was walking with Mum and my sister when I looked over to my left. I hyperventilated because there he was, the Steward, walking around town with his mates. I started to cry and wanted to yell out to Dad but what my mum said stopped me in my tracks. Her words were, "Shut up, don't say a word. Your dad will kill him and we will never get to Australia." Mum's words made sense and I did not want my dad to go to jail. I didn't want to be the cause of our family not getting to Australia.

I was terrified, but I shut up alright. Dad had no idea what had taken place and I did not enjoy my day in South Africa looking over my shoulder all day, I could not wait to get back on the ship. Here again, I encountered the experience of parental conditioning, control and fear. See how easily it begins? Simple things like, "Do as you are told. Don't answer back. Keep your mouth shut," whether right or wrong.

Once back on the ship sailing to the next Port, I was so relieved that I would never see the Steward again. To this day I do not think he was dealt with, I think he was kicked off the ship and that was it. I bounced back and was able to enjoy myself once again on our trip, seeing flying fish and dolphins following the ship was such a wonderful experience for someone coming from an old cobbled street with no garden, grass or bathroom, to being on board a ship, travelling across the world. Wow, how exciting it was! Even though we were '£10 Poms' it felt like luxury.

I was also conditioned to love Rock'n'Roll music because my parents met at a dance in Wythenshawe and they used to Jive together. Not because they listened to a lot of music but because I asked questions about how they met and what it was like back then for them in the '50s. I also felt their fears when my parents talked about what it was like for them as small children living through World War II from 1939-1945, Dad being born in 1935 and Mum in 1936. I was able to imagine their situation and feel what it must have been like to carry a fear of death as a child at such young ages.

I would listen to my dad's stories of being sent to a farm to be protected because he was an only male child and the fact that, when he was allowed to return home, he hardly knew his father who died not long after my dad returned home. My dad was left with only his mother, and as he grew up, he wanted join the Army, just in case there was another war, which he did because his dad was in the Army.

I listened to my mum's stories of how her family was so big with nine children that most of the time they could not make it to the air-raid shelters. Her mother could not round everyone up on time, so mostly they would hide under tables and in the cellar waiting for the bombs to drop. I listened as my mum told me the story of how her best friend and her family were killed when a bomb was dropped on their home. How sad and horrific.

Both my parents grew up in poverty and lived on rations, and so they were conditioned by life, world events and family, because they had nothing, we had nothing. They didn't know a way out until the £10 Pom appeared on the scene and Dad took it by the horns. Were you ever told, 'You will get what you are given'? We were, that was the motto in our home as it was in many homes. I have said the same things to my children in the past and almost everyone I have known has been there too. We develop a poverty consciousness.

Before I go onto the next chapter, I would like to remind you, the reader that being conditioned is neither good nor bad. We all wake up at certain times in our lives, prompted by different events or situations.

Linda M Noon

18

Chapter Two: The Knowing

Intuition Is The Supra-Logic That Cuts Out The Process Of Thought And Leaps Straight To The Answer - Robert Graves

June 1971 we finally arrive in Sydney, Australia, and all passengers were taken to a Hostel, ours was called East Hills Hostel. We had a little flat to live in, our flat was situated at the back of the Hostel near a small river and the bush. The front of the Hostel housed larger families in tin Army Barrack type homes. We were fed in a canteen daily. I loved the pancakes with strawberry sauce. The good thing about the Hostel was all of the families were English, Irish and Scottish, so it was great for us immigrants to be around our own kind.

Mum and Dad both got jobs easily, and we were soon put on buses to be taken to our new schools. Hammond Ville Primary School. Prefabricated classrooms. Everything was good at first until the Australian kids started calling us 'convicts' and 'Pommie convicts'. I never heard of such a thing, and I had no idea what they were talking about. It didn't feel nice and I began to feel like I had done something wrong, so it was not uncommon for my brother Steve and I to wag school and go and build a den in the bush.

The bullying went on for some time when I was at school until I asked my dad, "What does it mean and why are they saying that?" Once he explained, I was okay with it because my dad told me to tell them, "If it was not for us and their ancestors, they would not be here." That seemed to work and soon I started making friends.

After a few months we moved to another Hostel called the Endeavour, we weren't there long either and the next thing, Dad got another job working for a firm called Nabalco. It was in Gove, the Gulf of Carpentaria, Northern Territory. We were given a fully furnished four bedroom house, there was no television and it was hot, the rent was only $10 per week too. The best part was when we arrived and started our new school there were kids from the Hostel that we had met before, so everyone knew everyone again and it was the same deal, English, Irish and Scottish.

I loved Gove. I joined the Brownies, had my first bike and lots of friends. The beaches were exotic, there were wild buffalo roaming around, highly dangerous. The land was owned by the Aboriginals, and some lived on a Mission, we had shared beaches and separate beaches. The Aboriginals were great the typical Aboriginal with spears and loincloths but friendly. After a few months, my hair turned flaxen from the sun. We lived there for just over twelve months then Dad wanted to move to Melbourne.

I was sad to leave there, but it was a great adventure again as Dad had decided to drive all six of us to Melbourne packed into his Holden Kingswood. We flew out to Darwin and had to wait for Dad's car to arrive via ship as there were no roads in or out of Gove at that time. Once the car arrived, we set off towards Melbourne on a six-day journey. Everything was just a massive adventure with my dad. We were seeing places we would never have seen if we had stayed in Salford.

1973 we arrive in Melbourne, Victoria. After a short stay with friends we moved into a flat on Cowper Street in Footscray. Mum and Dad got jobs again and we attended new schools. Not long after moving into Cowper Street I met a friend called Sheila Smith, we became best friends and we still are to this day forty-seven years later. We ended up living next door to Sheila, she had a huge family, they were from England, but Sheila's mum was Scottish. Sheila's brothers were Bikies in a gang called 'Critters'. We all felt safe.

When I was around thirteen, Sheila and I would be on a train going somewhere or returning home, and I would often look around the carriage at people. I started to notice if a man was looking at us I used to get this weird feeling. I cannot really explain it other than a deep knowing that the person wanted to do us harm. We often went on the train to the City on a Friday night as back then the shops were open until 9pm. We called it 'Late Night Shopping'. We just went to hang around near the bowling alley or pinball shops.

Maybe it was because I was becoming a teenager and the hormones were kicking in, I don't know, but one night we were on a train ride home, the carriage was full of people. I looked up and there was a male looking at us, he wasn't doing anything and he wasn't scary looking. I just had a thought that kind of spoke to me saying, "When the train stops, get off and run like mad."

Without question I would say to Sheila, "Don't look now, but when the train stops get off and run like mad." To which Sheila would always say without fail, "Why?" I would reply, "Just do it." So that is what we did, we ran as fast as we could and low and behold the male would be hot on our tails. Sheila could not run as fast as me so she would be yelling, "Wait for me." I would stop, grab her by the hand and literally drag her to keep up with me. We never got caught and we always made it home to safety. Sheila would ask, "How did you know he was going to chase us?" I answered, "I don't know, I just did. It was a feeling and a thought in my head and a certain look in the male's eyes." That kind of thing happened a few times.

One night it happened with a gang of males, I was fourteen and Sheila was fifteen then, but we always got away. Looking back now, I can say it was a deep knowing without question. If I had ignored it, I dread to think what may have happened to us, and maybe it was a Guide or Guardian. I don't really know, but I do know I really trusted it. Intuition, gut feeling, just knowing something was not right. There was a feeling of impending dread and danger with the knowing that we had to move quickly.

Another time we had been to Williamstown Beach on the old Red Rattler train, those trains were so old with the old seats and a rack to put your cases like something from the early 19th Century. Sitting in our carriage there was Sheila and I at one end and a male at the other end, he was reading a newspaper and he was holding it up over his face so I could not see his face. I got a feeling and I said to Sheila, "When we arrive at the next stop we should change carriages." Again, typical Sheila asks, "Why?" I said, "That bloke down there." Sheila says, "Looks like he's stroking a cat." Because the newspaper was shaking, with that Sheila began to walk down towards this faceless man even though I said, "Don't!" but off she goes. Sheila walked to him and swiftly came running back up the carriage to say, "He was pleasuring himself." Well not in those words but you get the gist. We had to sit in that carriage until the next stop where we quickly got off and got back on into a carriage where there were more people.

I would have to say that those times were where my Knowings began to develop, and it became a part of me. I always looked around like my eyes were scanning trying to pick up things. A strange thing for a young teenager to be thinking about I guess, but it felt very normal to me. It didn't feel weird and it didn't feel like a gift, it just *was*.

By the time I was fourteen, my mum and dad had separated in 1976, my mum took my sister Tracey and I with her. She left my two older brothers, Mick who was nineteen and Steve was seventeen, with my dad. Mum had found a flat in Yarraville. That was a very emotional and hard time, I was in high school and I was a huge Elvis fan to the point that the day Elvis died, I never went back to school, I was three weeks off turning fifteen. I could not face going back to school because there were some girls there that used to tease me about Elvis and frankly, I did not trust myself to not give them a beating. So I refused to go back and at that time you were able to leave school at fifteen anyway, which was my plan.

On April 25th 1977, it was my brother Steve's birthday plus a public holiday, Anzac Day. The reason I remember that date will become clear as I write this next bit. Mum had bought him a pair of jeans, and she asked me to take them to him, which meant I got the train then walked the rest of the way to Dad's house. The shops were closed except Chip Shops, I recall. So I jumped on the train and made my way to Dad's house. As I walked from the top of Cowper St towards Dad's, I had to cross Footscray Road, on the corner was a Chip Shop that was open, and I knew the owners.

I walked past the Petrol Station, there was an alleyway running behind it, and I saw a man walking. As I glanced his way, I got 'that feeling' but I continued to cross the road and the owner in the chip shop waved at me. I could feel the presence of being followed when all of a sudden, the man overtook me and because he did, I thought I was maybe a little paranoid. I thought I was safe because he was walking in front of me.

I had just arrived at a block of flats behind the Chip Shop, there was an alleyway in between. I still had several houses to walk past before I would arrive at Dad's. This man stopped and began walking towards me, he stood in front of me and asked me if I knew where the Town Hall was. I told him it was closed, but it is around the corner. He then proceeded to grab my right arm and twist it up my back, at the same time he was groping me and he slammed me onto the letterboxes of the flats. I remember the padlocks digging into my back as he then tried to drag me behind the Chip Shop into the alleyway.

My feet planted firmly on the ground like they were stuck inside cement blocks, and he could not budge me. I yelled for him to get off me but he wouldn't, then in my head I heard, "Scream as loud as you can." I took the deepest breath and screamed right into his right ear as loud as I could, and to my surprise, it worked. He looked me straight in the eye. He was a tall Aussie bloke, he grabbed me by the throat and he said, "You stupid bitch." As he threw me through the air, he took off running. I scrambled to my feet and ran. It was like my feet were not on the ground, I arrived so fast at Dad's place, bashing on the door crying and shaking.

Dad took me to the Police Station and we reported it. The Police asked me what I was wearing at the time, I said, "What I've got on," which was a smock top and jeans. They then put me in the Police car and drove me to every pub in Footscray, I had to walk into every pub with them looking for him, but we never found him. Dad took me back home.

The next day, Mum had to take me back to the Police Station so I could look through the mug shot albums. He was not in any of them either. The attacker was wearing a cream Aran knit jumper and checked pants like Rupert the Bear. A week later his photo fit, still wearing the same clothes, was in the newspaper only now they were looking for him because he had raped a Nurse at knifepoint. I felt very guilty for that Nurse at the time because I thought if I had not screamed he would not have armed himself with a knife. Even though I know that is not true.

I was back at the Police Station telling them that he was the one who attacked me. This time they brought out more mug shot albums but he was not in those either. I never knew if he was caught or not. I do know I was lucky. In hindsight, when he overtook me on the street, I should have turned around and gone into the Chip Shop, but I thought I was safe because he had overtaken me and was now in front of me, and so I believed in that moment my initial feeling must have been wrong.

Later in the year of 1977 Mum moved again into a flat back in Footscray, this time a boyfriend of hers moved in. I did not like him and thought he was a creep. By mid-1978, he had left her and moved on with another woman in Adelaide. Mum's reaction was that she was taking Tracey and me back to England. I did not want to go, I was turning sixteen that year and I would have been able to leave home. Mum made sure though that we were back in England before I turned sixteen.

We got a council flat on Painswick Road in Wythenshawe after living with an Aunty for a couple of months. By that time, I had turned sixteen and could not get back to Australia; we were never Australian Citizens. I was terribly sad and unhappy. The good thing about it was that I got to see my grandmother again and I also got to meet my Great Grandmother Betsy, who was a Psychic Medium. I loved going to visit Betsy because she would just look at people and read them. One day she told me that she could see a lot of blood coming down my legs, but not to worry because everything would be fine. I was sixteen when she told me this. She also said, "It won't be now. It's a long way away."

My Gran didn't like what Betsy used to do but I thought it was great. Betsy often got arrested and locked up for the night because of what she did, it was illegal at one time. Betsy used to say to the Police, "I knew you were coming. I'm Psychic." Sadly she fell over and broke her wrist which then turned to pneumonia and she passed away in 1979 at the ripe old age of 92 years old.

My Gran gave all of Betsy's Psychic stuff away, a Crystal Ball she gave to their hairdresser and most of the other stuff she threw in the bin. I wish I had gotten her Tarot cards. I got an eternity ring with most of the stones missing around it, and it was very narrow. I still have it to this day. I also have some plastic blue and grey beads Betsy wore when she went out. It must have snapped at some time because there is a hook and eye sewn onto the ends of it. I often look at the stitching and like to think of Betsy sitting and sewing it on. Betsy must have loved that necklace to have gone to the bother of sewing the hook and eye on.

I did not like being back in England one little bit. I was working and going to College because I refused to go back to High School in England. Around August 1978 I met a boy, he was the first person to befriend me in the UK, and we ended up courting until around May 1979. After getting home from work one day my sister Tracey told me, she saw him in the park on her way home from school, rolling around in the grass with another girl. He saw that he had been seen by Tracey and he kept away from me.

I was upset because I had a crush on him but I did not show it, I did not make a fuss about it, even though an explanation would have been nice. I thought, 'Bad luck,' it was not within my control what he decided to do. Then in June 1979, I found out I was pregnant, although I did not go to the doctor for six weeks. I can tell you it certainly did not go down well in my house, but I had already made up my mind, I was keeping the baby. Later that same day I went around to my Ex to tell him, Mum came with me. I told him I wanted nothing from him and I only wanted him to know. We were both very young.

Later that evening, after he had time to think I guess, he came to see me asking me to take him back for the baby's sake. I said "No," but it was a kind gesture though. I know he was trying to do the right thing. We did, however, remain friends and he visited often to see how things were going. In Feb 1980, at seventeen years old, I gave birth to a baby boy. I didn't know what had hit me becoming a single Mum so young. Later that year my Ex seemed to fall off the radar, he no longer visited, so I just got on with it. His life had taken him in a completely different direction, I guess. Though we have been in touch since 2003 on and off and remain friends to this day.

In 1981 Mum told me I needed to move out and I should put my name down for a flat with the Council. I didn't really want to because I was scared. Mum had said that it was not right for a grandchild to be brought up in the same house as the grandparents, and I believed her. I also believed she did not want me there. In August of 1981 I was offered a three-bedroom house with a garden. I was shocked because usually you only get a flat. I took the offer and soon moved in with nothing. I did get a Government grant to get second furniture and a stove.

It was a very scary time in my life, I had only just turned eighteen and I was a single Mum. The house had no heating but it had an open fireplace in the living room so my first night there I had to make a fire out of an old wooden crate and newspaper. Luckily the guy who delivered a new bed saw I had no heating with a baby, and he returned that night with some wood for me, which was nice. I did not sleep well there and often sat up all night until I heard the milkman doing his rounds in his milk float, the bottles of milk would rattle in the

26

crates. I would sit at the top of the stairs on guard with a knife, as long as my son was okay and got his sleep. It was in this house that I started to have dreams and experiences that I could not explain.

Sometimes when I did get into bed for a couple of hours, usually around 5am, I would experience a strong smell of roses and a feeling as though someone was holding my hand. I liked to believe it was my grandad, the one I lost when I was five. Grandad had a great love of roses and he also had a beautiful Rose Garden, I spent many hours with him in his garden helping him with the pruning.

From the day we arrived back in UK in 1978, I used to daydream all the time about coming back to Australia, I missed it so much. If I was out with anyone who had a car I would be the passenger and I would be in a full-on daydream, asking in my mind, "If I will ever get back to Australia, give me a sign." I don't know who I was asking. I would look at number plates for answers, that was way back in the 1980s before it became a spiritual practice to read number plates. I was doing then what seems to be common practice today only I did not know what I was doing, it just made me feel better and gave me comfort. Those experiences still go on to this day; they make me feel safe as though I am receiving guidance.

The next part about another incident I encountered. I was going to leave it out of this book for fear of ridicule, but after much thought, I decided to add this in.

During the winter and around the beginning of 1984 I was lying in bed, I always slept with my bedroom door open, and I had the street light from outside that used to light up the top of the landing, I also never closed my bedroom curtains. My bed was under the window and each night I would look outside into the row of houses behind me. I could see who was still up or not by their lights on in their houses and I could see where one row of houses ended and the next row began. There was a gap in the shape of a 'V' at the end of the rows, where I often looked into the night sky to see if it was cloudy or if the stars were shining. On my window ledge I had a clock, the kind with two bells on top for the alarm and it was a wind-up clock, very old-school with a loud ticking sound. I got used to the sound so really I never noticed it.

At some point I fell asleep, but I often woke and moved around a lot. It had been snowing and there was thick ice on the ground outside, the upstairs rooms were always cold. During the night, as usual, I awoke, turned over in my bed and looked out of the window as I stirred. This particular night, as I lifted my head to turn, I saw something in the night sky, right at the point of the 'V' shape above the rooftops of the houses. It was very large, filling the space between the gaps in the house and above and beyond the rooftops. I could not believe what I was seeing; it was a very large UFO just sitting there in the sky, no sound, no movement. There were lights all around it but one light was far larger and brighter than the rest. My heart began to beat so fast I thought it was going to beat right out of my chest. I was terrified and up until that day I had no interest in UFOs nor did I really believe they existed, but at times I had thought about the possibility of their existence.

My brain was scrambling for answers to what I was witnessing, I thought of my small son sleeping in the next room and felt I must check on him but I was scared to move in case they, whoever they were, could see me and beam me up. I slowly slipped out of my bed and I literally belly crawled across my bedroom floor to my son's bedroom. I opened his door to find him fast asleep. In his room there was a toy box and I knew he had some toy binoculars in there so I reached in and grabbed them. At the time it was very real and scary but writing this now I am giggling to myself at what I must have looked like, if they could see me they were probably laughing at me. I crawled back to my room and looked through the binoculars but they were useless, I saw better with my own eyes. What was I thinking?

I continued to stare at this craft under the covers of my blankets because it was so cold. I remember the time being around 3am and I remember thinking, 'I wish it was 5am,' time for when the milkman comes around. The noise of the morning milk float always made me feel safer because people were up and about. I had no landline at that time and so I could not call anyone.

I really did not know what to do but watch, it never did anything, it just sat in the night sky. After some time of watching this craft I became really sleepy and I fell asleep even though I had tried to fight it, it was overwhelming. I often wondered afterwards how come I was so scared but I still fell asleep, how could that happen? After some time I woke up again and as I woke the vision of what I had seen flooded back into my mind and I literally thought it must have been a really vivid dream. I looked back at the window and, 'My goodness, it is still there.' The fear came flooding back, my heart beating out of my chest, my breathing short and shallow I almost wanted to cry with fear. Again as earlier, it did not move nor make a sound.

I watched again for some time and again I fell asleep but the next time I woke up I heard the milk float and quickly looked out of the window and the craft was no longer there. It was almost daylight and I scrambled out of bed, ran downstairs and put the television on convinced it will be all over the news. There was no mention of it. I put the radio on, again no mention of it. Surely I could not have been the only one to have seen this.

Once my son woke up I got him ready, put him in his stroller and off I went running to my mum's house where a brother and my sister Tracey lived. I arrived there banging on the door trying to explain to them what had happened during the night but to my disappointment, they laughed at me. Tracey said, "I believe you but it just sounds funny." So I never brought it up again for many years, because of their reactions I thought no one would believe me.

I do not know why that happened to me or why I was the one who saw it. I now definitely believe in UFOs plus the other reason I decided to write this into the book is because I have a feeling that now, during this Covid-19 Pandemic, there are going to be more and more stories that will come to light. Maybe even the proof that they do exist and it is not a 'conspiracy theory'. What I witnessed was certainly no conspiracy theory, that is for sure. I know what I saw.

Later in 1984, when my son began prep school, I got a cleaning job at Wythenshawe Hospital. I did not like it much, the cleaning was fine but I did not like disturbing the patients to clean as some of them were in a very bad way and the other cleaners were far from friendly, so I left after a few months.

In 1985 I got another job at Manchester Airport as an Aircraft Cleaner, that is where I know Ted Exley from, who inspired me to write this book. I enjoyed that job a lot, the people were good to work with and we all had many laughs. There weren't many women on the shift I was on which was a good thing because all they did was gossip and make trouble. It was very busy as one plane after another dropped we were sent out in a van with teams of four or five to give them a clean before the next lot of passengers got on board for their outward bound holiday destination.

One day when I was at home vacuuming I kept getting a vision in my mind, it was clear as day. I saw a Police van and car driving down my road and stopping outside my house, every time I saw this vision my stomach turned over, it made me feel quite sick and nervous. I had a landline then and when it rang I would jump out of my skin, and again I would see that vision. This went on for over two weeks. There was a man at the Airport who was very funny, George Burton, he asked me one day if I was okay so I told him what was happening and I said, "I think the Police are going to be coming to my house." He said, "They probably won't. You must be worrying over nothing." 'Maybe,' I thought, but it was that 'knowing' feeling again, only this one was really intense. Something did not feel right, and my stomach was flipping over.

I remember it was a public holiday, 'May Day' in 1985. I was almost 23. I was lying in bed when I heard a noise downstairs. I got out of bed and looked through the lace at the window at the top of the stairs, there in the front garden was a man holding an extra-large screwdriver, tapping it on his thigh. He looked up at the window and I know he did not see me. I jumped back and began to panic as I heard noises downstairs. That night I had put the telephone in the hallway for some reason unknown at the time. I slowly crept down the stairs and put my ear to the door, I could hear loud rustling but I thought the noise was in the living room. I had a huge hook on the door that was on, so I knew whoever it was could not get into the hallway.

I pulled the telephone as far as I could up the stairs and began to telephone the Police, in my panic I kept ringing the Australian emergency number 000 and got nothing but a silent tone. I began to panic more as I thought my telephone line had been cut. Then I realised what I was doing and dialed 999. The Police answered and I was whispering, "There is someone in my house and someone in my front garden." The Officer asked where I lived and I told him, he said, "We'll be there soon." I put the handset back on the receiver and crept back upstairs to check on my sleeping son. I also got my knife from under the pillow and I sat and waited for the Police to arrive thinking that, if the intruders do manage to get in the hallway and up the stairs, I will have to stab them, to protect my son. I felt sick with terror, and I could hear my own heart beating so fast.

All of a sudden I heard vehicles screeching to a halt outside my house, I looked through the window at the top of the stairs to see my exact vision I had been seeing in my head. There was a Black Mariah and a little white Panda car, out jumped the Police armed with Alsatian Police dogs. I ran down the stairs and opened the front door. The Police ran in with their dog and into the living room, we heard banging on the locked door to the kitchen and the Officer with me was kicking at the kitchen door, when we finally opened it with the key there on the other side was another Police Officer, both had thought that there was still someone in the house on opposite sides of the door.

31

The burglars had escaped over the next-door privets and into the avenue over the back. The Police found a sleeping bag in the garden with a video recorder in it, which was not mine because I had no money to own one. Fortunately, they took nothing from my house because I had nothing and the noises I had heard were from the criminals ruffling though my kitchen cupboards. My fault was that I had left the backdoor key in the lock and that is how the one in the kitchen escaped. If I had removed it like I usually did, he would have been trapped and caught in the Kitchen. There would have been nowhere for him to run but he had already opened the back door before looking in the cupboards.

The police were great though, they stayed with me for the remainder of the night until daylight, by which time my sister Tracey and my brother-in-law Eric had arrived at my house, and they stayed for a week just in case the burglars came back. Eric nailed down the windows after that but we had an emergency escape in case of a fire upstairs in my son's bedroom. They never came back but that night I armed myself with baseball bats and hid them around the house. The feeling I had experienced stopped and so did the vision. I knew then that I was being forewarned and if that ever happened again, I must take more action.

In 1987, Friday 13 February to be exact, my eldest son, who was six years old at the time, almost seven, had to go into hospital to get his tonsils and adenoids removed. I had talked to Tracey a few days before telling her I was really worried about this, but she made me feel better about it with her reassurance.

Arriving at the hospital he was placed into his ward with three other boys who were getting theirs out too, so there were four boys all being prepped for surgery. One by one they left the ward, all us mothers were told to get a coffee from the canteen because the boys would be gone for a while.

After our coffee we returned to the ward and waited, soon one boy arrived back, then another and another, sleepy in their beds recovering. I continued to wait for my son but he never came back, I was worrying and spoke with the ward Nurse who assured me he will be back soon, the wait felt longer than my labour. Finally he arrived and was placed in his bed, still sleeping. I sat beside him stroking his hair, full of relief he was back. The Nurse told me he will probably sleep for some time, so I walked a few metres up the ward to ring my mum to let her know he was okay and he was back in his bed.

As I ended the conversation and began to walk back I heard people running behind me and a voice yelling for me to get out of the way. As I looked over my shoulder, I saw four medical staff in their theatre scrubs running as fast as they could in my direction. They zoomed past me, straight into my son's ward and straight to his bed and quickly pulled the curtain around. There was great urgency and panic, as I approached I was stopped by a doctor who grabbed my arm and hurriedly marched me away around a corner into a Parents' Room and locked the door, I was crying my eyes out. I had no idea what was going on but I remember dropping to my knees and praying to whoever to take me and not him. I knew it was serious.

Finally, the main surgeon Dr Salam came in to see me and explain what had taken place. Dr Salam told me that my son had a respiratory arrest a few times in the Theatre and when he got back to the ward, but he was now stable. I asked him if it was going to happen again to which he responded by shrugging his shoulders and said, "I do not know."

Upon my return to the ward I was surprised to see my son sedated, a tube down his throat wearing a heart monitor and his bed was elevated so his feet were higher than his head. On top of both of his feet were puncture wounds, I don't know why he had them and I never asked. I sat at the head of his bed stroking his hair and talking to him as he slowly regained consciousness pulling out the tube from his throat. He was distressed, but okay. I slept there at the side of his bed on a piece of foam for a week.

The following evening I had a meeting with the doctors who had revived him and they told me that the reason he had a respiratory arrest was because the pack had slipped into his throat, at the time I accepted that, but it did not make sense as to why he had a few respiratory arrests. I did not care, as long as he was alive and okay. On the second day, I realised I missed my dad who was in Australia so much and I just wanted him to be there. I asked for signs to let me know my son would be okay. At first I received none.

Later I saw a newspaper near the bed and even though I never read the newspapers, I opened it up at the page where it was advertised what was showing at the movies at that time. What jumped out at me was nothing short of a miracle.

There in big words, it was written:

Friday 13th
Jason lives
Part VI

I had received my answer, that was a 'wow moment' because all of the above took place on Friday 13th, my son's name is Jason, and he was six years old! It could not have been any clearer to me. I tore the notice out of the paper and kept it with me, I had that clipping for many years but lost it somewhere along the way.

Finally, after a week he was allowed to go home. That was a very traumatic time for us both but fortunately he did not remember much about it, other than he is not fond of hospitals or needles. He also remembers they made him eat bags of chips and cold hard toast so his throat didn't scab over, when I had told him beforehand he would get lots of jelly and ice cream, I did not know they no longer do that.

A few years later he fell off a slide and broke his wrist, we ended up back at the same hospital in Emergency, they were going to take him into surgery that evening until I told them about the respiratory arrest he had at age six. The nurse had found him a bed but they could not find his medical records at all, he was born at that hospital too. I said to the nurse, "Oh, how convenient." It was then I knew that something had gone wrong on the 13th February in 1987 for his records to be missing from the system. The surgery for his wrist had to be put on hold until the following day as the nurse told me, because of his respiratory arrest they would have to wait for the top surgeon to do the operation and create a new hospital file. They even allowed me to accompany him into theatre wearing disposable scrubs until he had passed out.

These snippets of my life are stories I have shared to help others come to a realisation and awakening of the innate and dormant 'knowings' I believe we all possess and it appears that it is more active in times of trouble or foreboding. Some may call it a sixth sense.

Linda M Noon

Chapter Three: Fine Tuning

When Your Intuition Speaks Listen Closely And Follow

In 1987, whilst still working at the Airport, I met a guy I will call Carl (not his true name to protect his identity). My first impression of him was, I didn't like him, it was the same as in the past, something to do with his eyes. I did not think much of it and we worked in teams so it was no big deal. Carl had been working on the night shift and that is why I had never met him before.

One day we got talking as it was a bit quiet at work, not many planes were dropping so we had plenty of time to talk and we often had two or three teams hanging around in the crew room. When it was quiet we used to play cards, Black Jack, to pass the time. It was fun, and we all had a laugh with the jokes that would fly around the room. As Carl and I were talking, he began telling me stuff about his life and at some point I felt guilty for not liking him when I very first saw him. I felt I had judged him for no reason. Over time we became good mates.

Sometime in mid-1988, a couple at work were getting engaged, Frank and Mandy. Everyone at work was invited to their engagement. Carl had asked me how I was getting to the function, I told him, "On the bus." He then offered to pick me up and take me home afterwards which I thought was nice. So I accepted because I really did not know where I was going. Anyway, the night arrived and off we went, it turned out to be a good night. Afterwards, Carl dropped me at home. Not long after that he told me he liked me and I was taken aback but flattered as I had not really thought about being in another relationship. To be honest, although I never liked him at first glance, he had grown on me and we were friends, so I agreed to go on a date with him.

Actually, it was Frank and Mandy that were also behind us going on a date because we went on a double date, a day trip to Wales. It was a great day and we all had so much fun. We ended up in a relationship and later on in the year, Carl moved in with me and my son. We got engaged, everything was moving so fast, and I got swept up in it all. For the first time since 1978 I felt happier than I had previously been. We had arranged to get married at the end of September 1988, just a simple Registrar wedding.

Carl had asked me if I would ever have another child to which I said, "No, I don't think so." But he persisted in trying to change my mind, which I did. I got pregnant three weeks before our wedding. I was so happy. I almost gave up on my dream to get back to Australia but then Carl said, "I would love to live in Australia too." So that was the plan.

Before we got married we had been to Chester for the day when I came across this amazing shop that sold Tarot Cards, I bought myself a pack of the Rider Deck and I used to play with them when I was on my own. I learnt the meanings of the cards but only thought they didn't really mean anything.

Everything was plodding along nicely in my life. I was heavily pregnant around March 1989 and I began to not feel too good. I had pain below a lot which I never experienced with my first child. It even hurt when I walked. One night I had a dream that I was carrying a baby in a baby bath full of water down the stairs from my bathroom and as I did the front door opened and my dad walked inside looking up at me. My dad did not live in UK; he was still living in Australia, alive and well. As I looked at my Dad in the dream, the baby turned into hot coals in the water and melted through the bottom of the baby bath. I knew there and then something was not right.

I went to the Doctor and told him of my concern, I did not tell him of my dream for fear of being labelled crazy. He told me the pain was normal and he said, "This is what we call the Tidal Wave, the waters splashing against your womb." I thought that was strange but accepted it. I knew I had an appointment coming up at the hospital soon, so I thought I would mention it there.

38

In April I went for my hospital checkup, we did not get what women have today, we never knew the sex of the baby or 3D scans. I saw my doctor at the hospital, it was a woman and I asked her if she would give me a scan as I thought something is not right. She refused, telling me, "You don't need one."

In May I went into labour at 2am and went to the hospital, women gave birth in an operating theatre back then. Things were not right and I could feel it. I wasn't dilating enough, the monitor they attach to me to monitor the baby was erratic. Finally a nurse said, "We are going to break your waters." They told me it would not hurt but it did. They covered me up afterwards and left the theatre, Carl was with me.

Suddenly I began going deaf and the radio that was playing in the room went into slow motion, the voices were all slow motion and it was driving me nuts, I began feeling extremely lethargic and the pain of labour had stopped. I began to fall asleep, looking back now I was slipping into unconsciousness. I finally relaxed to sleep and I got the most excruciating pain like I was being stabbed. I screamed and a nurse came running into the theatre.

The nurse lifted the blanket and ran out only to return with an entourage of doctors who prodded and poked me and low and behold, there was the doctor who refused to give me scan a couple of weeks earlier. They had broken the placenta thinking it was my waters. I had a condition called Placenta Previa, meaning the placenta was coming out first, so I was actually bleeding to death and my baby had gone into fetal distress. I ended up in Theatre getting an emergency Caesarean. We both survived but there again the experience of the dream told me something was not right, that deep Knowing and fine-tuning had begun to filter into my dreams.

After seven days in hospital we were both allowed home, which was a relief, but then I remembered my great grandmother's words from 1979 about the blood and realised that related to what had just happened. A week or so after I returned home, I noticed Carl was not the same, he had become distant and it confused me a lot. I remember telling my mum how much he had changed and she said, "Maybe he is jealous of the baby, some men get like that." I told her, "Maybe he is." I tried to be extra nice to him to make him feel secure. Nothing seemed to work. So I just got on with it.

One night I had another dream, I dreamt that Carl was sat on a couch very similar to the one we had but a different colour, he was wearing jeans and a white grandad shirt with very fine stripes, the couch he was sat on was under a bay window. At the time he had changed his shift at work to two days on then two nights on and four days off. When he was on the night shift and the children were in bed, I used to get my Tarot cards out and ask what was going on. Every time without fail I turned over the Tower Card, which to me meant catastrophe, danger, lies, manipulation, deceit and so on. I never mentioned the dream to Carl or anything about the cards.

I got really sick a couple of weeks later with a bad flu, and my doctor had given me some antibiotics, during the day Carl said he would come home at midnight to take over with the baby so I could get some rest. I thought that was nice. Midnight came and went, it got to about 3am when I decided to ring him at work to see where he was. The Night Manager answered and I was shocked to hear that Carl was not in work and that he was on two weeks leave. I was shaking with fear over what was going on, then I remembered my dream about the clothes and the couch. I went to the wardrobe and looked through and the clothes that were in my dream were missing. I knew there and then what he was doing.

Around 5am he arrives 'from work' in his work clothes. I confronted him about where he had been, and he told me he had been driving around all night depressed. I tried to help him by not making accusations and I felt sorry for him. He then went on to say that he was going to stay at his dad's for a week or so to get himself right. I reluctantly agreed. Carl told me that if I needed anything to call him at his dad's. One night I called because I had run out of baby formula, I did not drive at the time. So you can imagine the shock when Carl's dad said, "He doesn't live here." My head felt battered. I was so confused and hurt but I could not get to the bottom of it all. Carl arrived at the house the next day, I told him I had rung his Dad, to which Carl replied that he had slept in his car, but I knew that was a lie, mainly because as I passed him in the kitchen, I smelt a pillow scent. I said, "Then why does your head smell like a pillow?" It just came out of my mouth, a strange thing to say, but the smell was really strong. After that Carl came back home only to disappear every day at 3pm and not return home until midnight.

There was a day I tried to prevent him from disappearing at 3pm, but he got violent and I had to escape the house. I ran up the road and he began to chase me in the car. He caught me around the corner and we began struggling in the street, but a stranger came out of their house and took me inside their home. I began to have a massive panic attack because he had my baby in the car with him. I could not breathe. Thankfully these strangers were wonderful.

All of a sudden Carl was back at the strangers' house with my mum in his car. I ran out telling Mum he had become violent and I had to get out, to my surprise Mum turned on him and began punching him. What a carry on that was! I got my baby back and began to walk home carrying my baby in my arms. Carl followed in his car, no matter how many times I told him to go away. Carl had told my mum that I had lost the plot and I had gone crazy and he didn't know what was wrong with me. What a lie!

Long story short, I was walking to the shops one day when I ran into a guy who also worked at the Airport, Eddie. We stopped for a chat, I asked Eddie if anything was going on at work because Carl was not himself, Eddie said, "No," we parted ways and I carried on shopping. Later that day there was a knock at my front door, it was Eddie, he came to tell me that he felt bad for lying to me and, "Yes, there was something going on. Carl was seeing a girl at work." Eddie gave me her name. I found her in the phone book, so I knew where she lived. I arranged for my mum to sit with my boys while I went around to this house, which I did. The girl's mother answered the door and I introduced myself as Carl's wife. The mother said, "You'd better come in."

Boy, did I get a shock when I saw their couch! It was exactly the same as my couch but theirs was blue and it was placed under their bay window. We had a good talk and the girl was very embarrassed and sorry because Carl had told her we were separated, plus a massive amount of other lies. She promised me she would end it and we promised each other we would not tell him about our meeting. She kept her promise, and he come grovelling back to me. He had no idea that I knew or that I had met with this girl. So he thought that we would just carry on as normal like nothing had happened, which is what I tried to do but I couldn't. I tried for my babies.

I found a job, opened a bank account, saved like mad for eighteen months, got myself strong, learnt to drive at age twenty-nine and booted him out. I bought a little car, took my boys to Ibiza for two weeks and had a great time, thinking I will never be put into that situation again. Then I divorced him, it was a DIY Divorce. Again my dreams had not let me down, even though Carl tried very hard to convince me I had gone crazy.

Funny thing was Carl had even managed to convince the doctors that I was nuts, they sent a Psychiatrist to my home to assess me. Fortunately for me, the Psychiatrist saw through him and she went back to my doctor and said, "There is nothing wrong with her, it is him." The lesson here for me was, that I should have trusted my first initial reaction to him the day I met him and thought I did not like him, there was something in his eyes, but I ignored it. I ignored my intuition.

I know that there is an innate force I cannot explain, it is powerful but subtle, sometimes heavy and all-consuming, and sometimes like a gentle breeze brushing across your cheek.

From everything I have learnt from those times, I know no one can lie to me because I will find out very quickly, my feelings, intuition and dreams will tell me. They may get away with it for a short time but not for long. I also know that I will not bat an eyelid in removing you from my life, as hard as it may be or how painful. When I see those signs I will walk away. For my own sanity and soul's growth. Not one person does everything right in life but you cannot keep doing everything wrong either.

Linda M Noon

Chapter Four: It Gets Better

Don't Just Wish For A Better Life, Go Out There And Create It
- Joel Brown

Fast forward to 1995, around the back end of 1994, England has just begun to roll out the Lottery, and we never had anything like this before in the UK. I never played it because I never had any money. In May of 1995, I had three dreams at different times of receiving a cheque for $5,000. One I remember very clearly was of my friend Jacqui running up my stairs while I was in bed and yelling, "Here's your money," while handing me a cheque.

I was in a relationship at this time with my best friend Sheila Smith's brother Glen who had moved back to the UK in 1979. Glen had moved over to the other side of Manchester in 1980 and had been in a long-term relationship, which came to an end. My family never saw him much during those years but he had arrived back on the scene and we ended up in a relationship in 1993. It was something I fought against because I had known him since 1973. Glen and I were getting married on the 23rd June 1995, nothing special, another Registrar ceremony. Everything was booked for that date.

On June 14th 1995, I was at my local shopping centre as usual daydreaming about going back to live in Australia but wanting it more than ever as my oldest son was growing up too fast and he was fifteen at the time. I remember the weather as cold and grey even though it was supposed to be summer. There was a feeling of despair in me too. I always felt pissed off, sick and tired of being in the UK.

As I passed the Newsagent's who did the Lottery I got a very strong feeling to go inside and play the Lottery for Saturday 16th June 1995, but I didn't have much money as it cost £1 a box of six numbers, I had £3 left in my purse. The feeling was too strong, and I went inside, asked what to do, and proceeded without thinking about numbers to fill in three boxes. I more or less filled them in out of anger and frustration, got my ticket and went home.

On Saturday 16ᵗʰ June 1995, Glen and I were at Stockport Shopping Centre, we had gone to get our wedding rings engraved ready for the ceremony on the 23ʳᵈ June 1995. After a day walking around the shops, we headed home on the bus. Later that evening after dinner I was taking down the numbers of the Lottery and proceeded to check my ticket, Glen was in the kitchen. I yelled, "Glen, I have five numbers." I began to get really excited and so did Glen, I stopped myself though from getting too carried away as I thought, "Knowing this scabby country, it will only amount to £200." Later on my eldest son came home and I told him I had gotten five numbers.

Early the next morning my son ran to the Newsagency to ask what the prize amount was for five numbers was. When he arrived home he told me it was £2,655. I did not want to believe it because in my dream I received a cheque for $5,000 and converted into pounds, that was close to what I had won!

Glen said, "We can have a better wedding now." To which I replied, "No way, that money is going towards getting back to Australia, I am not spending a penny of it on the wedding."

On the Monday, I took my younger son to school and I had planned to go get my winnings. When we arrived at the school it was closed because someone had set it on fire over the weekend. So I continued to take him with me, I had to get a bus to Altrincham Post Office. When I produced my winning ticket, I was told that I could only have £200 in cash and the rest in a cheque, so there appeared my cheque. We quickly returned to Wythenshawe so I could put the cheque in the bank.

Shortly after I sent off for the Immigration papers and began to set the wheels in motion. I was worried we might not get back in. A week later I received the papers back in the post and someone had sent fresh papers with a sticky note attached that said, "Apply under Former Resident 151." I had applied under Family Reunion. I reapplied under Former Resident 151, I had to send proof I had maintained contact with family still in Australia, school records, telephone bills and letters. After I provided all of that, I sent the paperwork back to the Australian Consulate with a fee of £297.

The weeks passed by with no contact from the Consulate. We were beginning to get worried as four months had passed with no word. One night after the boys were in bed and Glen was at work on a late shift, I was sitting in the kitchen at the table. I do not know why I did what I did next but I got a piece of paper and pen and decided to try to do some Automatic Writing with my eyes closed. I scribbled on the paper 23rd November and some illegible gobbledygook. I put the piece of paper in a fruit bowl I kept on top of the microwave and forgot about it.

My dreams had become more vivid and I had a lot that were about being back in Australia. One that still stands out in my mind was that I was driving a red sports car with the top down, on the back seat were the old-style suitcases that were made of really hard cardboard. I was driving in the dark up a dirt road.

In October 1995, I received a letter from a specialist practice in Manchester with an appointment date for the four of us to go for a medical. Guess what the date was? 23rd November 1995. I scrambled looking for my piece of paper with that date written on it. It was a really strange feeling to see what I had written months earlier but also very exciting, it kind of scared me a bit because I had no explanation how I could have been spot on with the date.

After the Medical, Christmas came and went, I still did not spend any of what was left of the winnings at Christmas time although the temptation was there. I was hoping we would have heard something by Christmas so that we could relax.

January 1996 the new year started well enough, it was cold and had been snowing with a layer of ice on the roads and streets, my thoughts were, "Why was it taking so long?" Then on 31st January, Glen had left for work and he offered to drop my youngest son at school on his way so I could have a lie-in. Not long after they both left I heard mail coming through the letterbox of the front door and hit the hallway floor. I leapt out of bed and ran down the stairs to see a letter from the Australian Consulate which I still have in my possession to this day.

I was shaking with anticipation and overwhelming excitement plus some dread just in case it did not say what I wanted it to say. I was still in pyjamas when I ripped open the letter and there it was. 'We are pleased to inform you that you have been accepted to return to Australia under former resident 151' and something along the lines of, 'Get your passports and send to them to us so you can receive the visa to enter Australia'. It also mentioned that we had until November of 1996 to leave the country.

I ran from the house with the letter chasing after Glen before he made it to the School. I was slipping and sliding all over the street on the ice and it was so cold I could see the steam coming out of my mouth. I ran so fast and hard that I almost felt like I was going to have a heart attack with the pain I caused in my chest. The cold air made my bottom teeth hurt too. I threw a coat on top of my pyjamas and I was sweating like crazy when I finally caught up with Glen who had just dropped my son inside his classroom. I was trying to yell out to Glen but I was out of puff. Finally he heard me but by this time I could not speak because I was so out of breath, so I just handed him the letter to read.

Upon reading it Glen said, "Well, I am not going to work." We were so happy as we walked back home. As soon as we got inside I rang this airline called Britannia, it was only a small plane and I asked if I could book four seats one way to Melbourne Australia, the only seats they had left were on the 3rd March 1996, they informed me that was the last flight out until November so without hesitation I booked us on that flight.

We dashed about looking for our passports and I noticed my sons were on mine but there was a problem, my eldest son was turning sixteen the 27th February which meant he had to have his own passport and be taken off mine. This led to another mad dash to get the passports updated, back to me so I could send them to the Consulate, and get them back in time for the 3rd March 1996 as it could take up to six weeks to get a passport. Both my sons' and my passport arrived back to us just in time but only by the skin of our teeth. The Passport Office were great, though.

I then rang my sister, Tracey, and a few friends to let them know, even though it was a sad time they were all happy for us. Quickly I sold all my furniture and the last two days in that house we had to sleep on the floors on blankets. It was the best feeling I have ever had besides the birth of my children. We left on the 3rd March 1996 to board our flight one way with only a $1,000 on us.

We had family to live with for a short while when we arrived. I was worried about my eldest son because I had taken him away from his friends and I thought I may have done the same to him as my mother did to me when I was fifteen. Happy to report he fitted in well even though I know it was hard for him for a while, he has told me he will not go back to the UK as he knows which side his bread is buttered.

Sheila, Glen's sister, and I struck up where we had left off still best friends, like that saying, 'No matter how long or how far, true friendship picks up where it left off like you have never been apart'. I was so grateful and loving my life to be back home. Not long after in April 1996 we rented our first home, Glen was working and everything worked out so well and so quickly, just like it was 'meant to be'.

1997 I felt it was now time to focus on myself more and I decided to join a meditation class in a Crystal Shop in Werribee, I did not know what I was doing and I found it hard to calm my mind at first, but I soon got into it. Every day I decided to meditate at home, I soon got better and better at stilling my mind. I found a class to learn how to teach Reiki in Werribee and booked and went along to that, I did not really know what it was, but because I had been going into the Crystal Shop that also sold Spiritual books, I became curious about Crystals, Healing Methods and Angel Cards. One thing led to another and I started to meet like-minded people who I was able to strike up great friendships with.

My dreams were out of control at the time and very vivid, they were very bizarre, in my dreams I was meeting spiritual beings and all kinds of wonderful things were taking place. I was receiving a lot of what felt like teachings of spiritual knowledge and wisdom, sometimes geometrical shapes. I began to write Dream Journals. For some time I had seen a white tiger in my meditations and he always accompanied me, his name was Azar.

During one of my dreams I had seen that I was in Greece swimming in the ocean, there was a very handsome man there too, not of this time, he had long shoulder length wavy brown hair and a beard, and in my dream I knew him. The dream began to become recurrent and one night I asked his name, to my surprise he answered, "Azar". I thought, 'Wow! The same as my Tiger.'

Then he began to manifest into my meditations and he wore a long gown that was blue and greyish brown, a rope type belt tied around his waist. He told me he was from Atlantis and they were known as Altean's, and not Atlanteans. Azar called me Ilka, why I did not know at that time. I thought Ilka was some kind of a Deer. I did not have a computer or Google or a mobile phone at that time.

In a dream I was having one night many years ago, one of those electrical ones, feelings of being pinned down and dragged out of my body, I actually called out for Azar and without hesitation he appeared running towards me, his gown flowing as he got closer and closer. The electricity stopped and I began to relax and slowly woke up, I was facing the window lying on my left side and I physically felt a comforting arm around my waste, I turned to look over my shoulder and there was no one there. That was a bit creepy but I was not really scared because I felt very protected.

At some point, I do not know exactly when, I came across a crystal in a Crystal Shop that was the same colour as the gown Azar wore. I was very drawn to it because of the colour, so I inquired into what the crystal was called, to my amazement it was called Azurite, so of course I had to have it. That was an amazing moment where the hairs on my arms stood up.

Last night, in August 2020, after writing the above and finishing for the night, I decided to go onto Google to find out what the names 'Azar' and 'Ilka' may mean. I had never thought to do that before then, simply because I have not had Azar in my dreams or meditations for years, but this is what I found. Azar in Persian/Iranian origin means: Fire, or to shine and glow; Afghan: the ninth month of the year; Hebrew: Help. I was rather impressed with what I had found on the name Azar.

The meaning of Ilka was even more impressive considering I had taken it to mean a deer or some kind of animal that I guess I was mistakenly thinking of an elk. Ilka means: Torch, beautiful, light, bright and shining; from Ancient Greek it means: Sunray. I was amazed. These kind of happenings people usually refer to them as, Guides or Angels. Either way it is very comforting, and extremely subtle, during the waking state, as it allows your physical mind to accept what your soul, deep inner knowing or your higher consciousness already knows, your natural state of being is only supernatural to your everyday lower 3D mind.

Back in 1997, I began to see Aura's, I had to make a bit of effort to see them but I did see them. I completed Reiki I, II and Master/Teacher levels. I read so many Spiritual books and often I went along to a Spiritual Church in Williamstown where they would do readings and channel. I was not a fan of the Channeling because it scared me, I used to think what if something is trying to possess me. I did channel a few times involuntarily, it was so powerful because my left arm would shake, my heart rate would increase and my throat felt like it had expanded.

It was mainly all down to the meditation, as I had used to talk to myself and say I am filled with and surrounded by the Light of the universe, I am safe. I focused on my third eye area and over two or three months, I was able to still my mind and often be in meditation for an hour which felt more like fifteen minutes.

I was not into visualisation meditation as I thought and think it distracts you from the true meaning of meditation, which is to listen. I did not want to be disturbed by visuals, what would be the point of that, other than to distract my mind instead of stilling my mind. Visualisation meditations are very good though, for stress or just relaxation.

During meditation I would just look inside the back of my forehead and watch. There were spiraling colours, and now and then a face that I did not recognise. Sometimes symbols and Geometric shapes. Things that you could not possibly imagine, it was magnificent.

In nature, especially in rain forests, I could physically see what I called nature spirits, electric blue and vibrant green Orbs bouncing from one tree or plant to the other. This happened more at a place called Maits Rest just past Apollo Bay off the Great Ocean Road in Victoria.

In many of the books I read, the author always taught the reader how to protect themselves from lower energies or entities, to keep yourself safe from negative subtle unwanted energies, which have the potential to disrupt your mind or life. That also includes other human beings who claim to be Spiritual but they are not, they are called Vampires or better still charlatans. I have come across many people like this, you just know, you sense it and feel it. Your intuition increases when you learn to meditate correctly.

In 1999 I opened a Healing Centre called 'Chambers of Light' with a spiritual friend, Christine, in Werribee. Christine did not stay long and moved to Bendigo, so I carried on with the Centre offering Meditation Classes, Full Moon Blessings, Reiki Therapy, Readings as well as writing and facilitating workshops. I hired two of the rooms to other Therapists and I also sold some Spiritual retail items, such as incense, crystals and dream catchers, to keep the Centre going.

Monday, Tuesday and Thursday were the busiest days for Meditation classes, Saturdays were more workshops for Reiki Initiations and hands-on practices. Sometimes there were workshops about the healing energies of crystals and Reading days. After the meditation classes, the class would stay behind to have a coffee and chat amongst other likeminded people to share their stories. It was a safe environment without judgement or ridicule about spiritual experiences.

Thursday classes were held in the mornings for those who could not make the evening classes, it was an amazing time. One day after one of the classes, 28 November 1999, I was locking up getting ready to leave for the day when over and over in my mind I heard a female voice tell me I could not go until I drew her, even though one I could not draw and two I had no idea what she looked like. Eventually, I found a large piece of paper, some pastel chalks and blue tack, so I placed the paper onto the back of the kitchen door and began to draw in chalk, beginning with eyes. I was quite amazed at what I drew because it was the first time. Then I began to channel. Her name is Rowena having had a life in Wales and France, Rowena often said to me, "We are one," that took me a few months to figure that one out, but when you move the letters around in her name they actually spell 'we are one'.

Rowena is an Ascended Master on the 3rd Ray, High Priestess of the Temple of Light. Sisterhood of the Rose. She often spoke to me in French although I do not know any French. I still have the original picture I drew and a smaller version and a revamped version of her. It was a great comfort to have Rowena around.

I left Rowena blue-tacked to the door for ages, no one really noticed her, but one night after class one of the students told me she saw a lady in the room wearing a pink robe, I showed the student the picture and she verified it was her that she had seen. That made me feel good knowing it was not only me. Not long after that I began seeing faces in my mind all the time and continued to draw them, once I had drawn them, they seemed to become a part of the classes, guiding me into what to say or do.

Later that year, I met a Buddhist Monk, although I do not know how I met him. Master Venerable Thang, was a Senior Abbott. I went along to one of his classes and absolutely loved it, the Master was funny and taught me a lot. When he opened his Temple at the top of Ballan Road Werribee, it was not long before I told my Spiritual friends who also joined his weekly classes every Sunday for us Westerners. Buddhist Meditation is very much like what I had been practicing without knowing I was doing it.

Master taught us Mantras, Sutras and Buddhist Philosophy. I went to his classes for three years and often he would give us essays to do and mark our work. We would then receive a certificate and sometimes a prize. Once or twice a year he would take us to visit many other Buddhist Temples and now and then we all went out for dinner. We had a retreat at his Temple where we all took the Vow of Silence for 24 hours. That was a test I can tell you.

The Master would often talk about Human Superpowers that we all possess but because of our conditioning and our minds we do not believe and it is nothing special to them, it is a normal state of being. Enlightenment is the goal, the journey is the gifts we all have. When you become enlightened, you do not have to be reborn into this world of suffering and therefore step off the wheel of Karma of birth, death & rebirth. If you chose to come back to help others you are known as a Bodhisattva of Compassion and Mercy like Quan Yin.

At the end of 2001, I closed the Healing Centre down to return to study, I went to college to become a Clinical Hypnotherapist and at the end of 2002, I received my Diploma. During the time after I closed the Centre down, I hired rooms around local Werribee businesses to continue running Meditation Classes as my clients requested of me. After receiving my Diploma in Hypnotherapy, I hired private rooms to build a clientele, I enjoy Hypnotherapy because the results have been amazing for my clients.

From around 2000 onwards my dreams became more and more profound and I began to question a lot of events that had taken place around the world. One such event was the landing on the Moon of Apollo 11 in 1969. My husband Glen was a huge fan of the Apollo Missions, he owned all the videos and he often spent hours in the garden looking at the stars through his telescopes because of his enormous interest of Astronomy.

In 1986 when the Challenger Space Shuttle blew up, I recall thinking how strange that they could get to the Moon in 1969 with the materials they had then, but not now, in 1986. It has been reported that there were six screwed landings between 1969 and 1972. But I did not give it much thought. Then there was the Space Shuttle Columbia in 2003. I just could not get my head around it because of the materials and technology we had after 1969.

None of it made sense to me and so I decided it was all made up bullshit. Sometimes Glen and I would debate it, as he really believed they landed on the Moon and I didn't. It did not affect my life one way or the other. Over the years though I have heard many theories about it being a hoax, I also began to watch theories on how it was made in a Hollywood film studio. Personally, I still tend to believe it was a hoax, mainly because of what I had thought about it in the past.

I was still meditating and having prophetic dreams and inexplicable experiences and I was enjoying it so much. My intuition had grown to the point that when I knew something to be Truth every hair on my body would stand on end even in the midst of long hot summers days. This is known as 'Clairsentience', one of the many Psychic abilities, it can be a blessing and a curse because you feel everything, especially other people's emotions. You can sense a presence of energy in a room. You pick up a vibe about places, objects and people. You may experience a feeling of being drained of energy if you are around negative people or places. This can be very exhausting as well as exciting.

This next story is one of my favorites and it is still so vividly imprinted in my memory...

In September 2001 I decided to visit my dad in Gympie, Queensland for Father's Day for two reasons, one it was my birthday on the 3rd September and two it happened to fall on Father's Day. Dad and his wife Diane lived on their own property in the bush, it was a lovely little patch of paradise. Glen, my youngest son and I flew up to Brisbane, caught a coach to Maroochydore where Dad picked us up. Dad's house was only two bedrooms so Glen and I had to share a room.

The day before my birthday which was Saturday, Dad had taken us out to Tin Can Bay to take us in his little motorboat, he loved to show off and he was loving our company. Not long into getting into the boat and out on the bay, the boat stopped, something to do with the spark plug. Dad managed to get it going again and we decided to come back to shore. I didn't mind because swimming around in the shallow waters were two wild dolphins. I ran into the shallow water to get a closer look and to my surprise one of them swam towards me, as she approached she turned onto her back and I got to stroke her. It was something I was surprised to feel because she felt like wet fur. Then her baby came up to me, which was covered in scars. Dad told me that the baby had been caught in fishing nets.

Just behind was a little kiosk that were selling dead fish, so I went and bought one to give to the dolphin, as I approached her I was attacked by a pelican who managed to steal the fish away. I bought another fish and this time the pelican did not get it. It was quite funny because I freaked out a bit when the pelican swooped. Dad thought it was very comical. There was a man standing on a wharf who yelled at me not to touch the dolphin because I could give it a disease. I told him where to go.

Soon we headed back to Dad's place for tea, having had a wonderful day. Later that evening I developed a rash on my torso all down the front and down my back, I had a bit of a temperature too, but nothing too bad. Sunday was a great day, Dad had bought me a pair of dolphin ear-rings for my birthday and we celebrated my birthday and Father's Day. It was a great time.

Monday 4th September 2001, we were due to return to Melbourne, so on the Sunday night after our celebrations, I began to pack our bags ready for the following day and our journey back home. Finally retiring to bed, I do not recall the time but it would have been early because we had to get up at 6am, so that we made the return coach in time in Maroochydore back to Brisbane Airport to catch our flight.

During the night I had a dream, I was at the airport with Glen, in the centre of the waiting area there was a large glass cabinet with what looked like a mini-city, with an airport runway in the centre. I was looking into the glass cabinet looking at the miniature city, which was alive with people, like I was looking into their world but hey could not see me. I watched a plane take off, it was an American plane with a large 'A' on the tail. As I looked up to tell Glen, I saw a plane taking off on the runway in our Airport with the same 'A' on the tail and I watched it, all of a sudden the plane dropped out of the sky and into the city. I was shocked as I gasped a deep breath and I said to Glen in my dream, "My God, did you just see that?" In the dream Glen replied, "No."

At that point I woke up still at my dad's house and the room was filled with light and I felt a presence behind me standing in the room. I looked over my right shoulder and I saw a golden figure with golden light emanating from it. I remember thinking, "No! It's daylight already," I felt like I had only been sleeping for a very short time. I buried my face into the pillow and went back to sleep. Not long after that I woke up again and it was still dark. I lay there trying to make sense of what just happened and I was scared because we were going on a plane that very same day. My mind was racing as I thought that day was going to be our last day and our plane was going to crash.

Finally the sun rose and we all got up. I did not tell anyone what had happened during the night. I remember feeling really sad and I had a strong feeling not to leave but I could not tell anyone as I had no desire to scare anyone, especially my son. I was angry at why I had that dream right before we had to get on a plane to go home. Later that morning after breakfast we left to get the coach and say our goodbyes.

We boarded our flight and I can tell you that I prayed all the way home, I repeatedly chanted what the Monk had taught me over and over in my mind. Every little bump in the air I panicked inside and I kept looking at my son thinking how much I loved him and I was mentally surrounding him in light and protection and spreading that out onto everyone in the plane. I was mentally imagining angels sitting on the wings and flying under the wings to keep us in the air. My biggest fear was on the take-off and then I was thinking about the landing when we arrived back in Melbourne.

Finally we began to descend into Melbourne airport, what was only a two hour flight felt like ten hours, my heart was racing as I closed my eyes and gently continued with my Chanting, until we made a smooth landing, the relief inside me was unbelievable. I still did not mention anything until we arrived home and my son had gone out to catch up with his friends.

I began to tell Glen what had happened during the night, he said, "Thank goodness you did not tell me." We both had a little laugh about it but I still did not feel right in my gut about it, I felt incredibly sad, I felt like I was in mourning. I could not understand what my dream meant, or why I had physically seen the golden glow of the angel in our room that morning. What did the capital 'A' mean on the tail of the plane? I convinced myself the 'A' meant 'Australian Airline', then it changed to 'America Airline' until I then thought it meant 'Angel'.

This was Monday 5th September 2001, and those sad feelings stayed with me all of that week. I could not wait to see the Monk on the following Sunday for class, 9th September 2001. During the week I had cried in the shower to find relief from my sadness, I never mentioned anything to anyone because I did not know what it was all about and I was a little afraid that they would think I was nuts. I could not erase the dream nor the feelings, and I kept seeing it over and over in my mind. I knew the sadness was not mine because my life was fine, I had nothing to be sad about, but I did know that I was feeling a collective sadness. When, what and where I did not know.

Eventually, Sunday arrived as I got ready to go to the Temple I was re-running the dream through my mind, thinking the best way to tell the Monk and the class without appearing crazy. After arriving at the Temple and completing our class, I told the Monk what had happened and I told him how I still felt very, very sad. The Monk felt it was something that may happen and the dolphins may have been an ancestor from a past life. Buddhism is really big into past lives. He said, "Don't worry, you will be ok," with a smile. I did feel better, maybe because I had shared it. By Monday the feelings had lifted.

Monday night and Tuesday night were my main two classes for meditation. After I closed the Centre up and returned home on the Tuesday night, I arrived home around 10pm, everyone was in bed. I put on the TV but I had the volume down, I saw on the television planes flying into these two tall buildings but I payed no attention at all. I actually thought I was a movie.

I finished some paperwork and went to bed only to get up to the news the next day and see what I saw in my dreams. I was in a bit of shock and I burst into tears. I could not believe it, my mind was reeling, especially when it was mentioned that terrorists had done it. That did not ring true for me and I did not believe it. Somewhere inside I felt that was not true. For weeks that was all we heard about and eventually I accepted terrorism but not 100%. Who was I to question what the news and experts had to say?

Slowly, slowly though over the years there have been theories and documentaries about it, but I do believe it was an inside job. The problem is that if you voice what you believe you get labelled a nut job or a 'conspiracy theorist' and the way we get attacked is venomous and makes you feel like you have done or said something wrong for having your own thoughts, feelings and opinions. Anyone who goes against the MSM or the so-called experts are not tolerated, which is why most people stay quiet. We are brainwashed into believing the news is 'truth' and that they would not lie to us. We are controlled by the Global Elite who wish only to push fear and control upon us.

Many years on, we are still faced with the negative, destructive nature of the Elite, the most powerful, richest people on the Earth, who's only mission is driven by greed and the need for power. All of my previous experiences were before Facebook, mobile phones and even the internet in my case. Unless you are fortunate to socialise in a group of likeminded people, how does it all make sense and fall into place? Fortunately, in these days of Facebook and the Internet it is much easier to find like-minded people and much easier to research and find the truth.

There have been many, many dreams and synchronicities on my path and I realise, mainly during writing this book, how fortunate I have been to have experienced so much. Everything in this book is only a quarter of what I experienced. The main downfalls for me have been that for some reason most of the experiences, dreams and visions have been of a negative context i.e. forewarnings, forebodings and unpleasant truths. I cannot help but wonder why it could not all have been about happy events, some amazing happy events have been shown to me but not on an equal scale.

In the next chapter, I want to share with you a transition that many have experienced that I can only refer to as 'The Dark Night Of The Soul'. I have read that we all go through it on a Spiritual level as we awaken, the only thing is, I have never met anyone who has experienced it the way I did, so I have been unable to share much of it with anyone.

At the same time, I understand no two people's experiences are the same as another's. Maybe that is to keep us in Darkness.

Linda M Noon

Chapter Five: The Dark Night Of The Soul

The Dark Night Of The Soul Where We Learn Who We Are
Without People Telling Us.

Still around 2001 and onwards, as I continued to practice my Buddhism and Spirituality, my dreams began to change and become more vivid and intense. I began to dream about friends or a family member passing away months and even up to two years into the future.

One night I had a dream about my sister Tracey in the UK. I knew she had Lupus and had been diagnosed a few years before. She did not die. The dream was of Tracey as a baby and she was knocking on my bedroom door, when I opened the door, Tracey was dragging herself along the floor towards me, groaning. That was all the dream was about but it disturbed me a lot.

I had a foreboding feeling about it not to mention a sense of urgency to see her, at that time I did not have any money to go to the UK to see her but I knew I had to. One day as I was walking past a Travel Agent's in Werribee, and I got a message in my head to go inside and book a flight. "The money will come," I was told, so that is what I did. I had booked it for six months into the future, having no idea where the money would come from. A few months later I got a cheque from the Tax Office, so I immediately went to the Travel Agent and paid for the ticket.

During a Meditation at home, I felt compelled to write after I had finished, what I wrote on the paper was that Tracey was not inside her body and I had to go to the UK to put her back in. I was instructed to go to a very mystical place called Alderley Edge, to Merlin's Well and get some water from his well.

I used to go to Alderley Edge a lot before I left the UK, the energy there is so mystical. Merlin's Well was a face carving in a rock that dripped trickles of water and it was inscribed, "Drink from here and take thy fill, for the water falls by the Wizard's will."

This well is hundreds of years old and is mentioned in a book: http://www.mysteriousbritain.co.uk/legends/the-wizard-of-alderley-edge/ if you are interested to look. There is a wonderful mystery surrounding the Edge.

When I arrived in the UK, I stayed a week with my friend Jacqui Storey in Wythenshawe, and I told her of my plan to go to the Edge. Jacqui laughed but she was into it even though she called me 'Loopy Lou'. I hired a car off we went, Jacqui brought a video recorder with her. When we arrived there it was foggy and the fog glided across the fields ahead, it was a lovely sight. We arrived at the well but there was no water trickling down. Jacqui was laughing as she videoed me and she was cracking little jokes. I said to Jacqui, "This is not it. It's not the right place." We decided to walk to the right up and down small hills and climbing across rocks, we stumbled upon a little wooden footbridge and continued into the forest.

In front of us was a large old tree with the base hollowed out of it, there was a groove in the rock nearby and there was running water rolling down the rock, not with great force, but we could hear it trickling. We saw it was landing into a trough made of stone. I began to get really hot even though it was mid-winter and very cold. I felt like I was channelling the energy. I said, "Yes, this is it." I collected some water from the trickle into a blue glass bottle. We spent the rest of the time sitting inside the old tree and taking photos as well as videoing.

When we had enough we walked back to the Edge and had a little explore in the caves, known as the Witches Caves, and then we went to this beautiful old pub for Lunch. I have all of the photos and still have the video. After lunch we headed back to Jacqui's to watch the video back, while we were at the first well the video had picked up a sound like trumpets, even though there were no trumpet sounds that we heard with our naked ears at the time. We kept rewinding it and playing it over and over thinking how weird it was. I was really excited and Jacqui proceeded to tell me that nothing surprises her when she is with me.

The following week I went to Tracey's house to stay for a couple of weeks armed with my Merlin's Water. I did not tell my sister what I had been instructed to do but I did offer to give her a Reiki Healing which Tracy accepted. As I proceeded, I placed one hand on her chest and one hand on her solar plexus and in my mind placed her back inside her body. Tracey was very relaxed and told me that when I had my hands placed where they were she felt a jolt like she had been hit with a defibrillator. I then placed some of Merlin's water on her forehead and I was so happy because I had not told Tracey what I was doing.

That was a really spiritual holiday. It did not heal her Lupus, but it did put her back in her body and I believe she had been outside of her body for a lot of years. All of that transpired from my dream and it was a dash of mercy.

At that time I also began to have very strange sleep before I went to the UK where, as I was falling asleep, I would hear a noise in my ears, like a loud buzzing sound which made me become conscious but paralyzed. I could hear electricity running from one ear to the other as though it was travelling through my brain, then I could hear and feel it running up and down my spine, it made me freak out because some nights I would see dark entities in the room.

One night I saw four of them, two were holding me down and the other two were trying to pull me out of my body. I would begin to chant or say the Lord's Prayer and as quick as it began it would stop. This did not happen every night, some nights my dreams were lucid, spiritual and prophetic as usual. I did notice though that it was happening more and more often.

On a Sunday afternoon after our class with the Monk I asked if I could speak with him privately, I told him what had been happening and he told me it was not good. I had to go with him and kneel in front of Buddha. The Monk brought out a Bagwa Stamp, I call it a Bagwa because it looked like the Bagwa Mirror, he told me it was over five hundred years old. As I kneeled in front of the statue of Buddha the Monk placed it on top of my crown and began hammering it on top of my head whilst chanting something in Vietnamese. He then drew the Om sign on a piece of yellow paper and told me to sleep with it under my pillow and if it happened again I had to tell him.

It did happen again and again and I told him another time, the Monk did the same procedure and this time drew two Oms on paper and told me I had to burn one at the front door of my home, which I did. It stopped for a while but soon came back. I tried to figure out if it was stress but I had no reason to be stressed. One of the dark beings looked like a Darth Vader.

One day the monk took us all out for the day to visit a Temple where all of the monks were women, I can't remember where it was only it was somewhere in Victoria, it was a lovely relaxed day. This temple had a little gift shop where they sold prayer bead bracelets and posters, all kinds of everything Buddha and Quan Yin. I bought a gold-coloured pendant in the shape of a heart on a red string. On one side of the heart was the Lotus Flower and on the other side of the heart was Sanskrit writing. I thought that would be good to wear to bed to keep me protected from whatever was happening to me in my sleep.

That night I wore the heart to bed and the length of the string that it was on rested nicely at my heart chakra. During the night I had one of those experiences, I heard and felt the electricity in my head and running up my spine, there they were again trying to pull me out of my body but I remained attached at the hips. My mind woke up fighting and struggling to be fully conscious and the heat in my body was out of control.

After I woke I grabbed my heart in my hand and asked, "Why? Why did that happen again?" As I grabbed the heart I felt it was no longer smooth, so I got up turned on the light and the lacquer on the Golden Heart had melted on the side that was closest to my skin. It freaked me out and I never wore the pendent to bed again although I still have it, I kept it as proof to myself.

It was not always a negative experience, sometimes I was out in the Universe mingling with tall Light Beings and being taught stuff of a Spiritual nature. One time I saw a Nun and began talking to her. I often would awaken in the morning with the words of the song by Led Zepplin 'Stairway to Heaven' running in my mind. I often saw Orbs of Light that burst in front of my eyes like when a child is blowing bubbles. They would get larger and larger, sometimes they were different colours, pale orange and blue and then they would pop. I was in awe of those experiences. I was given symbols and geometric shapes.

I had experienced Kundalini (Spiritual Awakening) on a few occasions way before I ever met the Monk which were totally involuntary, I did not know what was happening to me. During meditations I felt the energy in my base chakra, I felt it as a spinning ball and it was warm, then without warning it would rush up my spine, which caused my heart to race, breathing became faster and there was a slight vibration on my left side, I would go with it even though it was powerful and a bit scary, the heat radiating inside is a bit uncomfortable. I would look into my mind's eye and all I saw was light so bright but it did not hurt my eyes. Afterwards, I would feel totally calm and peaceful for hours.

I had been seeing Aura's around people for quite some time, not all the time and sometimes I had to really try but the best one I ever saw was the Monks. Every August the Temple celebrated a day called Ancestors' Day. There was a ceremony where the Monk would do a ritual of burning coloured paper, the congregation would bring fruit as an offering to their dead ancestors, they believed that on this day each year the veil between the two worlds was thin for the ancestors to receive food, money and clothing. After the ceremony, the Monk would release white doves. If our mothers were still alive we were given a small red paper rose to pin to our lapels, if our mother had passed, we were given a white rose.

After the ceremony, we all sat on a cushion inside the Temple and the Master would do a talk about our ancestors and karma, compassion, service and love. I was sitting up the back of the temple with my friends when I saw the Master's aura begin to expand as he talked about love. It expanded wider and wider, the colours were vibrant all around him, red, orange, blue, yellow more like gold, they were irregular in shape and size but spectacular, encasing his whole body. I do not recall what the rest of his speech was because I could not take my eyes off his aura. I felt calm and stunned at the same time all day.

Around 2003 the Monk asked his Westerner class if we wanted to be part of the Temple's Committee, we agreed because his own people had been stealing from the Temple. During this time we also took five Precepts and converted to Buddhism, after our ceremony we each received a certificate with our Buddhist name on it. The name I was given is AN'DAI. I did not realise at the time what it meant.

Not long after, the Monk moved to Newcastle in NSW to open a new Temple, he asked me if I would take care of his Statue on the Pedestal, which I still have to this day because he never returned. After the monk left, I remember having a dream about Princess Diana, she appeared sitting on the end of my bed, handing me a pink rose. I asked "What am I to do with this?" Diana replied, "Dry it, crush it and scatter it."

That was all there was to my dream and I had no idea what it meant. One day I was looking at my Buddhist name on my certificate and the name I was given ÁN DAI when it dawned on me, if I change the letters around it spells DIANA, that sent shivers up my spine. I still miss the Monk after all this time and I have tried to find him over the years but to no avail.

What I began to ask was, "Is the test of the Dark Night of The Soul about feeling alone, unable to discuss what I am going through in my sleep? Fear? Is it a test to cleanse fear away? Is it a test to stand in my truth and light? Is it the Darkness trying to stop me from attaining Enlightenment in this lifetime? Am I experiencing involuntary Kundalini whilst I am sleeping? Why are these things happening? Am I Mad? Is there something wrong with me?" I have never met anyone who could fully understand what I went through from time to time, even though I have the internet, I have researched many phenomena but still find no answers to what goes on with me. It would be great to find someone.

Most of the time it is few and far between because I do not meditate as much as I used to and maybe I should get back into it, only I can find the answers to myself and the true nature of consciousness or Mind. I have accepted myself as different and I still fit in, I do talk to my friend Sheila about stuff, even though she may laugh and we both make fun of it, Sheila never judges me, she just accepts, this is 'who I am'. I do still have prophetic dreams and waking experiences, I do still love to help people spiritually with whatever issue they may have and I feel I am a good listener.

I sometimes wonder if all of my experiences have been so that I may help others by being able to put myself in their position and their feelings through my vast life experiences. Good and bad. Even now as I write this I am having an epiphany that maybe those who come to me for help is because most life experiences are negative, most people are not happy and have suffered and do suffer in many ways throughout the day. Maybe I would not have been able to help if I had not experienced what I have in order to help others. I have not learnt from

69

a text book except the Hypnotherapy, but even that study is so close to Buddhist belief of the Mind and the power of the Mind.

Chapter Six: Merging Lotus

Intuition: When you don't know how you know, but you know you know, and you know you knew and that's all you need to know
- Zen to Zany.

As the years began to pass and life continued on, I still continued to meditate and often had the same experiences that it just became a part of my newfound me.

In 2005 my circle of Spiritual friends made a pact that we would go to Uluru for the Full Moon of May, Buddha's Birthday known as Wesak. Something we had all talked about but never did, until 2005. There was Rose, Lee, Elaine, Marilyn, Lauren and myself. Lauren was an ex-student and client of mine, but we struck up an amazing friendship. Off we went on our journey sharing a cabin with only two rooms, Marilyn, Lee, Lauren and I shared a bunk room while Rose and Elaine shared the other room.

This was a no-frills five-day trip. When we arrived Lauren put all of these braids in my hair, we were all like little kids. We went on a coach trip to the Rock and went inside the Dreamtime caves, each night we walked to the Pub to get dinner that you had to cook yourself on the many barbeques they had there. There would be a band playing. We had a good time.

One night we had decided to hire a minivan so we all put in and hired a van only to discover that we could not drive out of the vicinity, so we planned to drive back to the Rock the following day and find a spot in the shrubs to do a meditation. I was the designated driver, which was fun. That night I had a dream about an Aboriginal Elder, I recall we talked and talked but I do not remember the conversation, other than where to go when we get to the Rock.

Early the following morning, we set off to the Big Red Rock. I had told the girls where we were going to find the spot and they followed. After parking the van, we set off walking to the right of the Rock and walked and walked. Elaine had asked, "How much further?" To which I replied, "Only around the next bend." Suddenly, as we walked around the next bend there was a small opening into the shrubs and just below a beautiful spot, I looked at the Rock and I saw a little ceramic red five-pointed star placed upon a part of the Rock. Waiting for the others to come and see it, I said, "This is the spot."

We struggled through the shrubs and noticed that the trunks of the shrubs were black charcoal as though there had been a fire there at some time, so we decided to paint our faces with it. Lucky there was no one around, we would have scared them. We sat on the Earth of the base of the Rock and meditated, the energy was amazing, Rose and I took a turn of leading us into a meditation. A truly wonderful day. We did more meditations throughout our time there and the night of the Full Moon.

When our journey was over and it was time to return home, all was well in our worlds. Not long after Lauren found a small lump at the side of her ear, Lauren was referred to get it removed under anesthetic, but it would not stop bleeding and she was transferred to another hospital only to discover a few days later that she had Cancer of the Skull. Lauren had to have part of her skull removed and a titanium one constructed, the muscle from her back was to form part of her scalp and skin from her thigh to cover the muscle. A huge long process and lots of tears and suffering for Lauren. After that Lauren had to go through Chemotherapy.

At that time I was still renting rooms to continue to run my Mediation Classes and after Lauren began to feel better she returned to the classes. 2006/2007 Lauren had begun to be hopeful that her Cancer was gone and the signs were promising but during 2007 she was told it had spread to her lungs. It was devasting for Lauren and her family, and for everyone who knew her. Lauren was just a beautiful soul.

I remember that last time I saw Lauren, she had come to class and she had bought me a Blue Dream Catcher which I still have. After class that night Lauren stayed back to talk, it was lovely. Lauren made a joke that if there is anything on the 'other side', she will let me know. Lauren had told me that she knew she was going to die and she was not scared to die; the only fear Lauren had was how.

We used to have a private joke between us about the model Elle McPherson and we often laughed about it. We laughed about it that night. I cherish the last time I was with Lauren. In August 2007 I received a call from Lauren's sister Melissa, telling me Lauren had passed, I was in the bank at that moment. I dropped what I was doing and drove home crying my eyes out. Lauren was only 30, I was in my 40's. I cried as I drove to Werribee South to let Rose know, and after I left, I began to cry again driving back home.

There was a song out at the time that I did not like at all by Fergi, I don't know if it was called 'Big Girls Don't Cry'. Those words were in the song, but for some reason I began to listen to the words and through my tears I took it as a message from Lauren. I remember these lines, "I hope you know, I hope you know, that big girls don't cry. It's time to be a big girl now." And something about, "It's personal myself and I. The path that I'm walking I must go alone. And I'm going to miss you, like a child misses her blanket. It's time for me to go home. Don't cry, don't cry." I got shivers, not because of the song but because of the words.

It was almost dusk when I got back home and I went into my bedroom and sat on the end of the bed, the door was open and I had the laundry room light on and the ensuite bathroom light on. As I sat crying the lights began to flicker like Morse Code, I looked up and thought, "Oh they are going to blow." They flickered and flickered as I remembered what Lauren had said to me about letting me know if there is anything on the other side. I asked, "Lauren, is that you?" the lights flickered in response, then it settled down. I asked, "Are you okay?" the lights flickered. "So, there is something on the other side?" the lights flickered again. I felt a peaceful calm coming over me and the lights remained on, they did not blowout. Even though I was incredibly sad, I was able to stop crying and feel comforted in the words of that song and the lights.

That evening and a few nights in a row I dreamt of Lauren, she was sitting on a chair waiting and we talked and I remember in one of the dreams I asked her, "Why do you look like you, I thought you wanted to be Elle Mcpherson?" we both laughed. I was at peace with it because I knew Lauren was okay. Lauren's funeral was amazing; the Church was packed with people who knew her and loved her deeply. Lauren's mum, Lidia, even hugged me so tight and thanked me for taking Lauren on our trip to Uluru. Lauren was buried in Werribee Cemetery in a lovely spot, I used to visit all the time but then I stopped as I don't deal well with burials, I am much more likely to heal if there has been a cremation.

Around the end of 2006, I had a dream about my dad who lived in Queensland. The dream did not have much detail in it. I remember in it my dad arrived at my home, and he had driven from Queensland to see me, it was around Christmas time. He was knocking at my front door, and when I opened the door, Dad was standing there with his wife Diane, they had a black Jeep and it was full of Christmas gifts. There was no conversation, only the look on my dad's face disturbed me. The black Jeep bothered me and that was the end of my dream.

I woke feeling disturbed because for me anything with a black car or a black dog has never been good news for me. So I worried that something was going to happen around or just after Christmas time. Nothing happened that year but in 2007 my dad had sold his property in Queensland and took Diane and himself to the UK, Ireland and Spain for a holiday and he had bought himself a brand new Peugeot, the plan was when they arrived back in Australia they were to settle back in Melbourne. I had not physically seen my dad since Christmas 2004.

I thought it was a bit strange for Dad to have done what they were doing and often wondered what was going on, but he never let on about anything. I was happy they got to do what they did, even though the dream I had started popping into my mind. I had spoken to my brother Mick who lived around the corner from me and I mentioned something may happen. Once Dad and Diane were back in Melbourne, Mick and I went over to visit, they lived a good two to three-hour drive away from us.

Dad had been in and out of hospitals for little things we were not aware of because Dad played things down. Upon our visit to their home in Grantville, it was obvious to me that he was dying, he was so thin and he had an oxygen tube up his nose, he was able move around the house freely because the tube was so long that was attached to a machine. When we asked questions he did not give straight answers. A nurse came to the house to inject Heprin into his stomach. Dad told us only that he had developed blood clots in his lungs from the flight to and from UK.

I read the nurses chart and memorised the words on it. When we arrived back home I googled the meanings and it was not good, it was Cancer. I rang Mick to tell him as Mick did not ask too many questions and he thought Dad would get better. I told Mick he won't get better. Mick rang Dad to ask him and Dad said, "Where did you get that from? Linda?"

Not long after Christmas, Dad was rushed to hospital because he had a fall, so Mick and I were going back and forth to Grantville. I asked a male nurse what was going on and was told that Dad did not want anyone to know. I told the nurse, "I am not stupid. I know what is happening." Dad hung on for weeks and he was even very coherent right up to the day. He still made us laugh. He was incredibly brave and still did not let on.

When we arrived at the hospital, Dad would look incredibly angry, he would look at me happily then look above my head and his look would turn to anger. He had a bad habit of buzzing the bell for assistance and was often told off by the nurses but his attitude was, "That is what they get paid for." On the day Dad passed away Mick, Diane, Kerry and I were by his side. He was in some kind of coma, and it was not pleasant. Hours and hours went by and then on the 22/02/2008 in room two at 2pm, Dad took his last breath.

Straight away the buzzer went off in his room, the nurse came running asking, "Who pressed the buzzer?" none of us had touched it, we did not know where it was. The nurse found it in the top drawer of his bedside cabinet. A few minutes later it went off again and we all looked at one another and Diane said, "That will be your Dad." We all knew that.

Mick and I walked up the hallway as Mick wanted to use the payphone. I don't know why we didn't use our mobiles, I can't remember. As we approached the payphone, I went to lift the receiver when I saw a beautiful blue butterfly sitting on it. As I picked up the phone the butterfly flew towards the electric doors at the entrance and out into the street. I thought that was a sign form Dad telling us he was free and transformed. I know there were two tall light beings stood at either side of his bed head, I saw them during the night. Although I was heartbroken, I felt a sense of peace for him.

After Mick and I arrived back in Werribee that evening I needed to ring my sister, Tracey, in the UK. Tracey was unable to be with us during that time as all flights to Australia were fully booked, but Tracey had been on the ward phone with us during that time. As I was talking to Tracey on the landline I was describing to her what happened and answered any questions that she had, we were both crying on and off.

After we settled down a bit and returned to some kind of composure, I looked up and saw a beautiful electric blue apparition glide across the living room about eight foot in front of me. It was transparent inside the electric blue outline of a male figure but the transparency was like water suspended inside the outline. Very hard to explain, it took me by surprise and I gasped, "Oh, Tracey, you'll never guess what I have just seen." Then I explained to her what had just taken place. I knew there and then he was okay and that was his visit to me to let me know, it was not the only visit I had.

The following week at Dad's funeral I wrote a eulogy, I just knew it was the right thing to do in his honour. As I was reading what I had written, I looked up to thank Diane, Dad's wife, for all her care for him while he was sick. I saw my Dad standing at the back of the room with his suit on that he was cremated in. He was holding a cigarette and he was proud as punch, I can still see that image in my mind as clear as day.

One of the songs my dad had chosen for his sendoff was Josh Groban's 'You Raise Me Up'. I had never heard the song before that day, and after that day I heard it all the time, as soon as I hear it the hairs stand up on my arms and I always say, "Thank you, Dad." I take it as a sign he is around.

A few days after Dad's funeral I was lying in bed, the bedroom door was to the right of me and it was open. I was sitting up watching something on a small TV, the TV was in the far left corner when out of my peripheral I saw the exact same apparition standing in the doorway as I had seen in the living room about ten days earlier when it glided towards the TV on the far side of the room, I watched it as it disappeared once it reached the TV. It did not scare me, I just said in my head, "Thank you."

A friend and I decided that we wanted to learn how to make a Mandala a few weeks after my dad had passed, so we took a private class at a woman's house I do not recall her name. I ended up making a Mandala with a dolphin in it and I dedicated it to my dad. That night in bed I was just drifting into sleep when I saw in my mind's eye a white light in the distance, I watched intently as it came closer but suddenly it picked up great speed and came flying at me, it stopped right in front of me, and it transformed into my dad's face, he was wearing a white T-shirt with a red-ringed collar and he said, "Be careful." Right at that moment I jumped out of my skin because it happened so fast, it startled me. I said to him, "Don't come at me that fast, come whenever you want but be more gentle in your approach." I lay back down to sleep and I had lost the image.

In the morning I had arranged to go to Daylesford with my friend Marilyn, she was driving so I told her to be careful and I told her about my experience the night before. "Yes, I will," she assured me. We were travelling along when up in front of us on the opposite side of the road I saw a car coming, pulling a trailer behind it. Up ahead, there were two cars in front of us.

I saw a tyre fall off the oncoming trailer in the distance and it bounced across the road, two cars ahead of us. I thought it was going to bounce into the open field on the side of the road. It didn't, it hit an electrical post and flew through the air straight towards Marilyn's car. Marilyn had not seen it and I yelled out, "Slow down!" As the car slowed down the tyre skimmed past the driver side windscreen and missed us by an inch or two. "Oh, my goodness," we could not believe it, how lucky was that? I put that down to my dad and the fact I listened and took notice by staying vigilant but also because I associated the red ring around his T-shirt to symbolise 'HAZARD'.

2009 I continued to experience the electrical dreams and visions and at one point it was happening more and more, I decided to go to the doctor because I was beginning to think there was something seriously wrong me. Trying to explain what I was going through was rather hard as I felt incredibly stupid. My doctor sent me to see a Neurosurgeon, who after I explained to him what was happening and we had a couple of giggles about it, he told me that he was 99% sure I was experiencing sleep epilepsy, so he sent me to Royal Melbourne Hospital for some tests and a MRI.

I waited two weeks for the results, when I went back to see him, he told me that my tests were normal and that there was nothing wrong with me and the only explanation in his words were, "True psychic phenomena." He assured me I had nothing to worry about and he recommended a book for me to read called 'The Dweller on the Threshold'. He also asked me to send him the information I had written in my dream diaries, which I did. He said, "They will make great conversation with my colleagues." I still have that report too. He did offer to put me on a medication to stop the experiences but I declined, even though they are scary at the time, a huge part of me is curious to find out what they are one day.

In 2010 I was summoned to the Crown Court in the UK for a very serious court case as a witness. I did not want to go at all, the flight was booked for December 2011, and the court case was to be 2nd January 2012. At first, it was going to be a satellite link-up but the Court changed their minds and sent me a summons to appear, they bought the ticket for me to go. I won't complain about that because it was on the Emirates Airbus, that was a great flight even though I was scared of going.

As the time was approaching, I left my two grown sons to live on my own because I knew I would have moments of falling apart and I did not want my boys to witness their mum so upset. I moved out of home and got my own rental, just so I could fall apart in peace without tripping them out.

I began to have nightmares and often woke in the morning with bruises on my wrists and chest. I constantly bit my tongue in my sleep to the point I began to talk with a lisp because my tongue was so sore. As it got closer to the time I was supposed to leave Australia, I began having dreams about my dad. One dream was actually in the courtroom itself, my dad standing by my side, the person I was witnessing against came in and tried to talk to Dad but he ignored him. I walked in the court and, in the dream, my Dad said, "Ey up, here comes, Linnie."

With that the courtroom was in disarray and the perpetrator ran off. I woke the next day thinking it was going to go in our favour.

Another night I dreamt I was on the flight and my dad was with me, he was wearing a light blue t-shirt. Waking from that dream, I felt safe and okay about it, to the point I thought, 'I can do this, it is all falling into place.' There was a sense of calmness.

Then the day arrived where I had to leave Australia to go to the UK. I think it was 27th December 2011, I know it was after Christmas but before New Year. I was looking forward to seeing my sister Tracey because I had not seen her since 2003. Arriving at Tullamarine Airport I had at least two hours before I could board the flight, so I decided to hang around the duty-free shops and have a look around.

I had the old Nokia phone at the time and all we could do was receive calls and texts, not like what we have now with social media and internet. As I was walking around duty-free I received a text, it wasn't really a text but my phone went off like I had received a text. I reached for my phone to see on the screen 'Dad E 4', that was it. My hairs stood on end and I was excited because it made me feel so relaxed and calm about the flight and the Court. What was strange was the fact that I was flying on Emirates from Gate 4. I believe without a shadow of a doubt that was a message from my dad. How did the phone spell Dad? I still have that phone because I saved the message as a contact even though I no longer use the phone, nor do I know where the charger is.

After arriving in Manchester, I was greeted by my sister, I told her what happened at the airport and showed her the text. New Year's Day came and went, and we were due in court on 2nd January 2012, I was still calm about it. When the 2nd arrived, we were preparing to go when we received a call that the perpetrator had changed their plea and decided to plead guilty. We were delighted because that meant we did not have to appear in court and go through the whole nightmare, what a great New Year's gift plus I then got to spend the next two weeks enjoying seeing my sister Tracey and her family.

We had a really good time. The cold English Winter also blessed me with snow, we had amazing fun playing out in it. We also got to go to Liverpool and go to the Tavern. Soon it was time for me to return back to Australia, I was happy to get back and happy it was all over. I continued on with my life feeling at peace and happy with what had taken place.

In March of 2012, on my dad's birthday, I took the day off work like I did every year since his death to honour him. I was outside in the garden, there was a small path which led into the back garden, I had been talking to my dad in my mind, wishing him Happy Birthday and reflecting on our times together. I was making my way back inside when I looked down at the ground and near the backdoor steps I found a little pink heart, as I bent down to pick it up I found another two pink hearts. I was studying them as I knew that there were no children next door who could have thrown them over and I was in and out all of the time and never saw them before. I had been living in the house for two years.

Suddenly the landline phone rang inside and I began to run to answer it before it went to messages, but I was too late. The answering machine said I had one missed message. I remember the time was 3.35pm because that was very significant. Listening to the message there was nothing but static and some kind of music that seemed to be in slow motion, that was when I noticed the time of the message 3.35pm, I felt the goosebumps as my dad's birthday is 3/3/35.

I grabbed my mobile and I recorded the message on my phone, a couple of days later I went to visit my brother Mick, and I told him of what took place, he was freaked about it. I played him the message and he said, "I don't know what that is but I do know that the music sound is in the note of D." Mick is a musician. I replied, "Oh 'D' for Dad." We both laughed then but I again am convinced it was my dad in spirit trying to let me know he heard my birthday wishes for him. Sounds a bit nuts and a bit out there but that is how I roll with it all now.

One day after work I was on the Freeway making my way home, the traffic was starting to get to me after years of it being bumper to bumper and at least one crash a day. I had just entered the Freeway and seemed to be cruising along nicely when in my mind I asked, "Dad, if you are with me, give me a sign."

For at least five minutes I received nothing and continued travelling along when this elderly man in the right lane next to me overtook and merged into my lane in front of me, he was driving an old red Ford. I was driving along behind him when I happened to glance at his number plate and, "Oh my goodness." I could not believe what I saw, it made me very emotional as I said in my mind, "Thank you, Dad." The number plate read, 'Dad 335'.

I tried to follow this elderly man but I lost him by getting stuck at lights, I was able to see though that the road he turned down was called Tower Road. I tried to catch up, I even turned down that same road to look for him but he was gone. That was one of the most amazing instant clarifying moments for me. It always brings with it a beautiful sense of calm.

In 2013 I became a Granma for the first time, I was also present at the birth, it was scary but wonderfully magical. The year before my now daughter-in-law became pregnant, I had a dream that I was in a house with lots of windows, the sun was shining filling the room with light. I was in the living room and on the floor lying on blankets there was a baby, I walked over to see this baby shining light, especially from the brow area, he had a symbol on his brow the same as mine as we looked at one another the baby spoke to me telepathically and I back to him. I knew it was a boy. The following day I remember thinking about the dream and wondering what it could mean. Then I did not think much of it.

A few months passed into the New Year of 2013 when my daughter-in-law rang me at work crying that she was pregnant and could I leave work and go to her. Leaving work, I grabbed a test on the way even though she had done many tests that all showed positive.

When I arrived at her home, she did the other test and it was positive, but I was not allowed to leave until my son arrived home from work because she was too scared to tell him on her own. Finally, he arrived home and we told him the news, he took it well but at first he thought we were joking. So all was well. I thought of the dream I had the year before and in my heart I knew it was going to be a boy, I felt the soul connection and I was so happy.

Finally, the day arrived for him to make his entrance into the world in October 2013. It was such a joy, as the months passed, as he began to grow I loved to look at him with his white-blonde hair and piercing blue eyes, watching him develop his little personality. After his Mum went back to work in 2014, I used to mind him a couple of days a week, he was such a joy.

When he was around 8-9 months old, we used to go and lie down on a bed in the spare bedroom so he could have his afternoon nap but before he would settle he used to crawl under the blanket down to my right foot, he would hug my foot and often put my big toe inside his ear. It was funny, strange and very intriguing. I had a little tiny spot on the top of that toe that always used to itch but it was small, I never paid much attention to it. Over the months as my grandson continued to do his afternoon ritual, I began to take more and more notice of what he was doing and it got me to thinking I should go to the doctor.

He had begun to talk and often said he liked my feet, even though he only ever bothered with that one foot and toe. One day his Mum arrived to pick him up but he asked me to lie on the couch and put the throw cover over me, this was very funny because he told his mum she was not allowed inside and she had to wait outside under the pergola. We both smiled at this request but we did it anyway.

I knew he was wide awake Spiritually and I knew he was telling me something with his actions before he could talk. While he was under the blanket cuddling my foot and toe his mother entered into the living room and sat on the opposite couch waiting for him to finish his ritual, when he emerged full of smiles his mum said to him, "You are strange." He just smiled. I said, "No, don't say that."

After that I decided to go to the doctor without telling him what had happened, the doctor told me it was nothing and gave me a cream to try for a week. I told the him that if it did not work I would be wanting a biopsy if I had to come back next week. A week later the cream had done nothing, so I went back to the doctor who proceeded to give me a biopsy of the spot, not a pleasant experience, but it was okay.

I went back for the results a few days later to be told it was Cancer, a Squamous Cell Carcinoma and had to be removed as soon as possible. My doctor told me it was lucky I asked for a biopsy because this kind of cancer can only be detected that way.

He referred me to a specialist and within a week it was being removed. Now that experience was very unpleasant because it was done under local anesthetic and those needles going into the toe...Wow, did they hurt! I had four stitches in the toe for two weeks and was not allowed to get that foot wet, so you can imagine how awkward it was to have a shower, I had to sit on the floor of the shower with that one foot outside the cubicle.

Within a week the results were back that they had got it all and it had not penetrated the lower levels of the dermis. Without a shadow of a doubt, I knew that my grandson had picked up on that way before he could talk, and his actions were trying to heal it and let me know something was not right. It still blows me away now when I think of that time and if it were not for him, I would have continued to ignore it and ended up like Bob Marley.

Speaking of Bob Marley (a Reggae singer who passed away of Cancer of the Toe) the day I found out it was Cancer I told my friend Sheila and she was upset by the news, Sheila came to visit me that night and I made a comment to her about me being like Bob Marley, Sheila said the same thing and as we were talking about it, guess what song came on the radio…Bob Marley singing 'Don't worry about a thing, cos every little thing's gonna be alright', we both laughed. I took it as a sign for sure, it was loud and clear.

As the time passed my grandson stopped bothering with my foot, now he is almost seven but there is still the odd occasion when he has slept over that he has looked at my foot but never does what he used to do to it. He does still say though he likes my feet. He is a very special child and I know he will awaken again to the truths.

The above experience led me onto another path of getting heavily into 'Young Living Essential Oils' and becoming a distributor, I began an Essential Oil Course and set about making my own Sunscreen Lotions with High Factor Protection using Zinc Powder, Shea Butter, Bees Wax, Carrot Seed Oil and Lavender Oil, all therapeutic grade and passed by the FDA. Also Lip Balms, Facial Creams and HRT Lotions as well as Chest Rubs for my two beautiful grandchildren.

My grandchildren think I've got remedies for everything and often ask me for oils for something or other, and they even bust their mum's balls for her to call me for a particular oil at times. I love it, exposing them to this. I diffuse the Oils every day and also make elixirs with a drop of what is consumable to ingest through approved 'Young Living Oils' only.

I had dabbled into this in the past after a spider bite I had on my foot that took so long to heal with conventional remedies in late 2005. It would begin to heal and then flair up again and again for almost two years.

One night I had a dream after sleeping with this foot outside of the sheets because it used to burn. In the dream there was a man that I could only see from the neck down, he was Egyptian because he was wearing an Egyptian kind of skirt, he had incredibly muscular arms and was massaging my foot with some oil. I asked him what he was using and he said, "Coconut Oil, Lavender and Honey."

The very next day I made that oil and applied it every day twice a day, and to my amazement, it began to heal slowly and it stopped flaring up. I even told my doctor about the dream, and as soon as I told him I thought, "No! Why did I say that?" But he replied, "That's good. You must have been getting help from up above."

I always pay attention to my dreams, especially the Prophetic ones, I love dreaming. I pay attention to signs when I ask for one, and I usually get them in a cloud formation, feathers, butterflies, a song on the radio or a number plate. They come in many forms, even in flashes of inspiration to create a piece of art, poetry or anything creative. Even me writing this book whilst we are in lockdown for this Covid-19 virus. I want to be creative and not destructive in this time.

I have lived in fear with stress and anxiety in the last few years but when this virus hit, I actually became a much calmer person because we are all in the same boat. I did not feel so alone in my fears and stress and began my research into what is taking place now. I also began to understand what I have been feeling inside for some time which has been a constant feeling of foreboding but not knowing why.

In part two of this book, I will fast forward to the situation we are in right now and how I have come to my own conclusions about what I feel is going on. I may be totally wrong, or I could be right, either way, it does not matter because my whole purpose has been to share what I have experienced as being true for me. Some people may resonate with me and some won't. Some may think I am what they call a 'conspiracy theorist wearing a tinfoil hat', which I do not believe I am. I believe I am searching for the truth, and that truth is what resonates with me. Truth is what I feel in my heart. Just like all my other past 'knowings'.

I only want to share my experiences in the hope I can help someone else and maybe some will have experienced many things that are very close to my experiences and it will make them feel normal knowing they are not losing the plot, that is unless I have completely lost the plot. Either way, I am still functioning as a normal human being, mother, grandmother and friend so it really does not matter. I have enjoyed writing this in the hope others will receive enjoyment from reading it.

Linda M Noon

Part Two: Covid-19

Before I break this part down into Chapters, I would like to say again what I said previously at the beginning of the book. I am not an expert Scientist or Doctor and I do not believe in any way that I know better, because I don't. My wish is to share what I feel many people have, and that is the innate knowing that, "1+1 is definitely not equaling 2." Common sense is telling us that, if nothing else.

For a few years now I have suffered panic attacks and anxiety, they appeared out of the blue after I lost a couple of friends who passed away, I looked upon these people as some kind of support to me as I was to them. I went through a time of feeling isolated and alone, after sustaining injuries at work.

The panic attacks began while driving, why only driving I do not know, but when it happened it was one of the most scary things I have experienced, mainly because I was behind the wheel and I was responsible for my safety and the safety of others on the roads. Then it began on the Freeways, so I would find a longer way to drive around using back roads, it did not matter as long as I got to where I needed to go. Then it began on the back roads so I would find another alternative route which was even longer to reach my destination.

I began to get frustrated because I could not figure out why this was happening. There was a feeling that I was turning over to my right or if I was at traffic lights, stationary, the car felt like it was rolling backwards. These feelings would be the trigger to go into panic mode. Many times I had abandoned my car and left it, calling Sheila to come and rescue me. After it passed, I felt disorientated and foolish.

This got to the point where I could only drive a certain way and a certain distance which infuriated me too because I used to drive all over Australia, now I was confined to my area and all the backways I could find. After going for help I did not achieve the desired result I wished for, so I began to look for answers myself. I did all the usual stuff, began meditating again, relaxing breathing and so on. Unfortunately, nothing worked.

It is still only when I drive and no other time. I have searched my mind to try to find out answers to no avail other then I feel the horrid feelings of impending and foreboding energies of Darkness. I can feel the aggression on the roads from other drivers, as though they are in some kind of 'road rage' and I began to find it intimidating. If I go to a Shopping Mall I feel dizzy as soon as I walk inside, like I am picking up unwanted energies, it never makes me panic but makes me uncomfortable. I became self-aware to the point that I scan my body with my mind every morning to find out how I feel upon waking.

I am so sensitive to energy, even if I protect my Aura I still feel it. I look at the faces of strangers and can feel their anguish, whatever that may be. I am so aware of others' feelings just by a look or even a glance. I have gone through menopause without HRT, because it is made of Horse Piss, that is the short version.

I am getting old with the usual aches, pains and bulging discs, all the usual stuff that comes with age, as my ageing body reacts to this earthy environment, but you get used to that and get on with it. I still have no answers for what I feel and so accept it the way it is now. It is like what I had as a child but ten times amplified.

Chapter Seven: 2019-2020

A Year Ago Everything Was Different,
I Realise A Year Can Do A Lot To A Person.

2019 started off with lots of excitement, I love New Year's Eve because in my mind it is the only 24-hour window where almost every single human and country celebrates by cheering and feeling the love of welcoming in the New Year. I often think which is the first country in the world to kick off at midnight then which country is next and so on for a whole 24 hours. Strange way to think but I get really excited about this one night more than any other night of the year. I feel this is one day where we lift the energy of the world more than any other time.

I began a TAFE Course in February to study Business Administration (Medical) in the hope of changing career and finding a great job. I had been applying and applying, attending interviews but not winning the roles, it became increasingly clear I had wasted my time on the course because every job wanted at least twelve months experience in the role which I do not have. More than that though I could feel with each interview on first appearance I picked up the vibe that they were looking for someone younger, although they could not say that as it is unlawful, it was evident. I wanted a job by the end of that year.

In May 2019 Sheila and I did our usual trip to Nimbin to attend the weekend of the 'MardiGrass', a March to legalise Medicinal Marijuana CBD Oil. The energy up there is phenomenal, Friday night is 'Drumming in the Streets' and it is amazing, everyone comes out with their bongo drums and they just go nuts, you can feel the beat of the drum in your heart and know on a spiritual level you are receiving healing. There are people from all over the world that turn up for it. Everyone dances to the drumbeats.

We have met so many lovely people there being our fifth time going up there to far north NSW. Nimbin is set in lush hillsides and mountains surrounded by bushland and rainforests. A 40-minute drive from Byron Bay with its stunning beach and Lennox Heads where there is a spectacular Tea Tree Lake to swim in. We stay in a cabin surrounded by Rain Forrest, visited by kangaroos at sunset. The March is usually started off with the local Aboriginals' Smoke Ceremony, which I love. It's like smudging. There are bands and buskers, with the Combi Van Parade, not to mention the amazing food. It is just heaven. No trouble and no threat to your safety.

Besides that highlight, we knew once we get back home we had lots of tickets to go see bands and famous people and our year was pretty much planned out as usual. We had tickets to a Led Zepplin cover band, Engelbert Humperdinck, Beatles cover band, "Cool Change' a Little River cover band, Doors and Janis Joplin cover bands, the real Fleetwood Mac, Cat Stevens, you name it we've seen them.

Every Saturday we went out, dancing having fun meeting lots of new friends and no dramas. We knew we could not go to the MardiGrass in 2020 because Sheila had a wedding to go to so we planned for the Nimbin Music Roots Festival in September of 2020 and we always booked early. The year flew by as they usually do when you get older.

We had our Granma duties and seeing our children, going for meals and the usual kind of year, waiting for the next year to arrive so we could set off on our Road Trip and this time taking my dog, Choco, a brown twelve-year-old Chocolate Labrador. So the year 2019 was not that unusual from any other thus far.

On 29th November 2019 Sheila and I travelled over the other side of town to see 'Cool Change', and because it was quite a distance from where we lived, we decided to stay the night in a hotel right next door to the venue. We had travelled on the train then bus to get there, it was funny from the start because Sheila fell inside a lady's shopping basket on wheels on the bus when the bus moved suddenly. I could not breathe for laughing as she struggled to get out she fell deeper and deeper into the ladies basket on wheels, it was hilarious, still makes me laugh even now.

The night went well as usual, after the show we went back to our two-bedroom room with a balcony and sat listening to music and carrying on drinking because the venues finish too early. It was a warm night so being outside on the balcony was ideal.

Next morning we got up get ready to leave and go searching for some breakfast. After breakfast we organised an Uber to pick us up to take us home because getting public transport was something we could not face after a big night out. The Uber finally arrived and off we go heading home, the driver was Chinese and he had a cold so he was coughing and spluttering, I was sitting right behind him thinking, "I hope I don't get that."

A few days later, I started feeling rough, with a burning on the roof of my mouth, but no sore throat, then my nose. I was feeling like shit. After a few days, I started to feel better but I had developed a cough, very phlegmy and it hurt my chest when I coughed. This went on and on. I had made some antibiotics out of my pure ingestible oils; Oregano Oil, Lemongrass, Frankincense inside empty capsules. That illness, whatever it was, lasted into the New Year of 2020 but I recovered, it just took a while longer than usual.

Finally recovering, off we went out and about again like we did every Saturday. Sometime in February, we heard about this Wuhan Flu from China but nothing alarming to us. We did not really pay attention to it.

12th March 2020 we had tickets to go to Musicland to see a 'Pink' cover band. I can take or leave Pink, but Sheila liked her and I love all kinds of music, so it was a good change. We arranged to meet a couple of friends there and so that was the plan for the night. Turned out to be a good night, by this time we had heard more about Wuhan but still in Australia there were no dramas, no lockdowns or anything like that.

A few days after being at Musicland, I began to feel unwell again but nowhere near like I did in December 2019, it was just a cold. I decided to stay home anyway, just in case. I was steaming my head two or three times a day with boiling water and Young Living Eucalyptus Oil killing any germs that may be in my throat or nostrils because I had heard of this virus living up there. After a week I was fine but still isolated. I know there were definitely no lockdowns at the time because we were out on 12th March and Musicland was packed.

Not long after this the news was full of what was happening in the world with the Wuhan virus, Italy, Spain, UK and America. My first initial instinct was fear, thinking, "Oh my. What if I had that in December from that Uber Driver?" I freaked out a bit and speaking with my sister Tracey in the UK I begun to take this more seriously. I got up every day and put the TV on to catch up on what was transpiring in the world and it was horrific.

In Australia, though, we were still very lucky because the numbers were relatively low compared to everywhere else in the world. I figured it was because we did not have as many citizens living here. There were restrictions, like social distancing but we didn't have to wear a mask, in fact we were told not to because they don't work if you are healthy. You didn't need to wear one, and it would be a waste of a mask, according to Daniel Andrews back then.

I was keeping away from my grandchildren just in case, I did not want to get it and pass it onto them. Just before the end of March my eldest son asked if he could move in with me, I'm not sure why but I think he was more worried than he wanted to let on and it had been more than ten years since we lived together. I said he could because I had heard about lockdowns coming and I thought I may not be able to see him if that happened, he came to visit me every single weekend without fail before this Covid-19 arrived.

There was a lot of confusion and panic beginning to go down but not for me, as my anxiety began to abate for reasons unknown at the time. I thought during a time of worldwide panic, I would be worse but I began to relax, that felt and seemed very odd to me. Though a huge relief none the less.

Facebook was going crazy about it all with the story about the Chinese eating bats and the virus crossing over into humans. The Ruby Princess docking in Sydney with a number of cases on board. The world was going mad, it was just so crazy.

Stage 1 Restrictions took place 23rd March 2020, initially they went for four weeks at a time. Info on the restrictions can be found: http://www.gymnasticsvictoria.org.au/VIC/Posts/News_Articles/2020/Mar/Stage_1_restrictions_in_place.aspx

Stage 2 followed and even Stage 3. When I research the exact dates they don't seem to add up to me, I am sure we were not on stage three in March as I have found on the Internet. There were $1,652 fines being issued for anyone caught breeching the restrictions. Gatherings of more than two people were banned. No outdoor gatherings of more than two at a 1.5 metre distance from one another. Parks and playgrounds closed. Only allowed to leave home for four reasons: Work, Shopping, Medical or Care Giving.

The reason I do not believe we were in Stage 3 in March 2020 is because in May I went to a Protest at the Botanical Gardens and the only restrictions then were Social Distancing in groups of ten. The reason I wanted to go to the protest is because one, I felt compelled for my grandchildren and two, I had started to do some research into the yearly annual Flu statistics and discovered that many more contracted the Flu and many, many more died annually from the Flu each year than the Covid-19 worldwide, alarm bells began to ring out to me. I could not understand why our countries were being shut down for this.

I read about vaccines and what the ingredients were in them, all the poisons and not to mention aborted baby fetus. WHY? Why would they put stuff like that into a vaccine? I had known for a few years that vaccines were not safe but to what extent, I never really payed much attention. I know I have never given my dog a vaccine and he is a healthy twelve years old. I never got my cats vaccinated and they lived to be fifteen and only dying by getting run over. My children had been vaccinated but only because I was young and knew nothing better and I trusted the Medical world. I am not Anti-vax at all, I just want a *safe vaccine.*

Sheila and I got the train to the Botanical Gardens and I know we did not break any of the restrictions, as of that time protests were allowed as long as we were moving. The plan for that protest was to walk around the Gardens doing our 'exercising' in a peaceful protest. The protest was about Vaccines, Social Distancing, 5G, and taking away our rights. The protest was going well and we were all about to begin walking around the Gardens while social distancing, at that time we were allowed groups of ten, that's why I know we were not in Stage 3 restrictions too.

Police surrounded everyone on the lawn in a huge circle so we were unable to walk. Why? The speakers were threatened that if they used a loudspeaker, they would be arrested. Why? The speaker went on to speak using a loudspeaker and the Police allowed this to happen for at least forty minutes. We saw Channel 7 News there and other cameras. Everything was going well, then one of the Cops yelled out that we had to break up into groups of ten otherwise we will be arrested, the funny part was that the Cops were the ones who had forced us all together by circling us. Why?

At this time there were now three rings of Cops encircling us and Police on horseback. Again, why? The two outer layers of Cops had different coloured vests on. They moved in closer and closer towards us, trapping us in the middle of the lawns and with each step they took towards us in a very uniformed manner, they yelled from deep within "MOVE! MOVE!" Why? It was quite intimidating.

We all began to disperse and slowly make our way out of the Gardens heading back to get a tram into the City. There were no arrests and it was peaceful. As we were leaving the Gardens a nurse appeared in full scrubs and a mask on, Channel 7's Reid Butler was interviewing her. I overheard this nurse say, "It was a slap in the face for the frontline workers after all their training." I relayed it back to a woman standing behind me who happened to be a nurse and this woman said to the nurse being interviewed that she was lying and she said that she had seen her on the TV the week before without her scrubs on.

They had a few words, then I asked the nurse getting interviewed why she would turn up to a protest like this, being a one and only. Someone yelled she was a 'paid actor' who had been known to appear on the TV. She appeared at the end of this Protest and nowhere near where the Protest had taken place. So where did she come from? I believed she was a plant for after the event, for Channel 7. There was no trouble and no drama, everyone left the Gardens and headed home.

On the Six O'clock News that evening, there was a tiny bit about the protest and the headline read, "Police step in to defend a nurse being attacked by angry protestors." What? Sheila and I could not believe what we were hearing. We laughed at first. They played her interview and then the camera zoomed into the crowd earlier in the day and I know for a fact it was edited because right there, Sheila and I had been caught on camera walking around just after the Police stepped in to disperse the crowd earlier that day. We could not believe we were even in the footage because we had been careful not to get on camera but somehow we did. I still have that piece of footage too.

We both got angry at the false media and how they presented it to the public on the 6pm 'News'. We knew this kind of editing happens but we had never actually experienced it firsthand until that day. All it did to me was serve to be a catalyst to dig deeper into investigating the truth, trying to understand why the media would do such a thing. I had seen it the week before at a peaceful protest I watched live on Facebook, they did the same thing there and then embellished it all on the news later that night, but I did not think it would happen again so soon after that.

So my first red flags were those protests and how it was sensationalised for the nightly news. They even added footage from NSW of two people getting arrested and made it look like this all went down in Melbourne. Inevitably, the general public believed what they saw on the 'news' and were up in arms about the protests and so a 'great divide' began amongst the public.

Around March I had begun to follow the American President Donald Trump more closely even though he got on my nerves at times with his comments and his faces, I started to really listen to what he had to say and I started to like it, because I saw a man who was not afraid of speaking his mind as he began calling out the press as 'fake news'. So my investigations lead me down the path of American politics, even though I am not very savvy in politics, I was learning as I went along.

First, I began investigating statistics of the Flu and the death rates throughout the world. Then I came across other statistics about H1N1 Swine Flu, the Hong Kong Flu in 1968 that was happening during the time of Woodstock, the largest outdoor concert, and I asked myself, "Why weren't there any lockdowns during these times. Why wasn't the world in a Pandemic then? Why was there no social distancing then? Why was the World carrying on as normal back then?"

Nothing made sense. My mind was reeling with these discoveries as to, "Why now? Why has this Wuhan Flu taken a grip of the world but no other Flu had to the extent we are experiencing?" Closing down Economies, Schools, Small Businesses and livelihoods. The suicide rates doubled and not just in adults but in youth too, Domestic Violence, Child Abuse spiked.

- 1918 Spanish Flu killed 20 to 50 Million lasting almost two years.

- 1968 Hong Kong Flu estimated 1 to 4 Million deaths.

- 2009 H1N1 Swine Flu estimated to be 245,00 to 575,000 deaths.

- The WHO (World Health Organization) estimated that 250,000 to 500,000 died annually from the normal flu but this flu H1N1 never really infected anyone over the age of 60 years old. Why was this flu H1N1 attacking the younger generations?

- SARS-CoV-2 known as Wuhan Flu 2019-2020 at present, the word Flu is incorrect as Covid-19 is not in the same family as Influenza, and this one infects the elderly.

As it stands of today 7th August 2020 I have researched and found 712,334 Deaths and 18,986,629 cases. In comparison to the others, it hardly qualifies as a Pandemic to the extent of closing down the world. Information found https://en.wikipedia.org/wiki/COVID-19_pandemic

I was very suspicious about what was taking place in the world and soon realised that it was the year Donald Trump was running for another four years as President in November 2020. Was it all just a coincidence? I think not! It is not a conspiracy when you are beginning to join the dots. Things do not add up. America and the UK were absolutely flogged with this virus. Not to mention Italy. This virus attacking mainly the elderly and immune-compromised.

I watched the news everyday showing what was taking place in the world and it was shocking but I began to notice the specific words being thrown around. From the onset we were told daily the 'Covid-19' cases and deaths, then as our winter months began the wording changed to 'Coronavirus', I began thinking why are they now calling it the Coronavirus and not Covid-19? This puzzled me a lot, so I investigated the difference between Covid-19 and Coronavirus.

There is a huge difference. Coronavirus is the Flu and colds virus that we get annually, the two viruses are totally different, I started thinking the Media are changing the wording each day, one day they say Covid-19 the next day it is Coronavirus. I put it out there on Facebook and heaps jumped on my comment telling me it is the same thing. I knew it was not and proceeded to find links to the evidence about it. I also discovered that the WHO called it Covid-19 knowing it was SARS-CoV-2, they decided to call it Covid-19 so as not to cause panic throughout the world but it still caused panic anyway and mostly through the MSM (Main Stream Media).

I felt that this was manmade and it was aimed at America to take them down and destroy the World Economy because if Donald Trump does not get in again in November, the world as we knew it would be no longer. The world needs Trump to succeed. I felt China were behind this because while all this has been happening China have been busy buying up falling stocks and shares around the world and once this is over they will be one of the richest countries in the world and own land in every country. Is this a coincidence?

I also feel that Australia has been relatively lucky compared to other countries and my feeling is that China went easy on Australia because they already own so much in this country.

Our cause for panic here is relatively unfounded as 6 months into this Pandemic all other States in Australia except for Victoria are doing just fine, Victoria recorded on 10th August 2020 7,869 active cases 1,065 were in Healthcare. We had 322 new case dropping from 793 two weeks ago. There is also a new call for a new test program, In-home testing. WHY? Numbers are dropping. Borders were closed except between Victoria and NSW all the way through until 8th July 2020 when it was decided to cut Victoria off from all other States.

Linda M Noon

Chapter Eight: The Death Of George Floyd

Who You Are When No One Is Looking Is Who You Really Are
- Matthew Jacobson

On 25th May 2020, George Floyd, a 46-year-old Black American man, was killed by Police in Minneapolis, Minnesota. Police Officer Derek Chauvin, a White Officer, knelt on his neck for eight minutes. George was yelling he could not breathe and shortly after his body became motionless, he died later that day. George had passed a counterfeit $20 note in a store and apparently, he was drunk and not in control of himself. It took authorities a week to arrest the four Officers involved in his death by which time the general public had begun to riot in outrage.

The footage of what transpired was all over the News and Social Platforms like Facebook. There was public outcry that was soon followed by rioting, lootings and killings, and the carnage was in the headlines for a few weeks. America suffered another blow with all this, and a movement formed called BLM (Black Lives Matter) at first it was horrific to see what was happening in Minnesota.

Shortly after it began people were using the cameras on their phones to capture footage of what was going down. There were random white people dressed in black with hoodies and masks on, smashing windows with hammers. One piece of footage I came across was a young black male approaching a guy smashing windows and following him as he hurriedly tried to leave without being detected, the young black male asked him what he was doing and followed him around the corner. The white male pulled his jacket aside and the black male looked down at what I do not know, I suspected a gun, then the black male walked away. It was rather bizarre behaviour. A few days later, the white male was identified by his ex-girlfriend as a white Police Officer from another area. She had recognised him, and he was wearing her mask.

I started watching footage over and over, and other footage I came across on Facebook of men delivering stacks of pallets and bricks, placing them strategically outside shops and businesses during the night so that the rioters were fully armed for the next day of rioting. It just did not seem right. More and more evidence came to light about George Floyd being on drugs, he had committed armed robberies, held a gun to a pregnant woman's stomach, overall not a very nice person, but still that did not warrant his death.

What did not make sense was the rioters began destroying their own neighbourhoods and harming their own people, 570 businesses were destroyed. During the day the riots were peaceful but once nighttime arrived, it was no longer peaceful. There was a curfew but that did not stop what was taking place even though Minnesota National Guard were called in, it had no effect. Blacks were killing Blacks, yet it was supposed to be about Black Lives Matter. It was a total shit fight. It continued on, BLM protestors began ripping down statues of past slave owners, graffiti all over them and then the movement began to spread into over sixty countries like the UK, Europe.

It even started here in Australia but our protest was civil and it was more about Aboriginals that had died in Jails or lock-ups but again failed to mention that most Aboriginal deaths occur within their own communities by their own people. It happens in all races not only Black, and no, I am not racist. There are many injustices towards everyone from the Police Forces and rightly so they wanted 'Justice for George'. It was bedlam. We had black youths beating up white girls at train stations here in Australia and many other incidents like this. It seemed it had spread to our country but mainly amongst the youth who were cashing in on it.

The American Democrats gave George Floyd a State Funeral but at that time no other person was allowed to have a funeral with more than ten people. It just did not make any sense whatsoever. It felt like the Democrats were purposely trying to antagonise the rest of the population if not the whole world. Why did this man get a State Funeral? What had he contributed to deserve this? Not that I care either way other than, WHY?

Officer Chauvin was charged with 2nd-degree Homicide, Officer J. Alexander Kueng with aiding and abetting, Officer Thomas Laner aiding and abetting, Officer Tou Thao aiding and abetting for preventing bystanders from intervening. The first autopsies showed George to have heart disease, Covid-19, Fentanyl, Methamphetamine and Cardiopulmonary Arrest due to compression on his neck and was ruled a Homicide. The second autopsy found mechanical asphyxia, Floyd's death ruled to be a Homicide at that time in June 2020.

Another puzzling fact was that Officer Derek Chauvin and George Floyd knew one another, they had both worked as security at the same night club in the past.

It was not long before people in America and around the world were saying it was ANTIFA who were behind the riots in America, that they were being paid to cause as much unrest as possible. There was footage on Facebook of large BLM coaches bringing ANTIFA into the Counties, and they were being paid large sums of money from Soros. Soros is a law unto himself. Anti-Trump Hollywood stars and famous singers were paying the bail money for any of ANTIFA who got themselves arrested. They have also been calling to defund the police.

George Soros survived Nazi-Germany and has a net worth 8.3 billion dollars. A Hungarian-American born in 1930, even though described as being of Jewish descent, he was often labelled Antisemitic. He has been a Democrat for thirty years. Some say he is on quest to destroy America and he does not like Trump. In recent years Soros has tried to take over local law enforcement agencies and quietly take down Donald Trump.

Soros now wants to move onto Education of the Youth to train the next generation in the evil of sovereignty, to teach the emerging youth how to become good obedient citizens of the World. If successful, it would mean the collapse of borders and the implementation of a World Government and the end of life as we know it because what happens in America happens everywhere in the Western World.

Some say Soros should be charged with War Crimes because he apparently watched the Jews during WWII and reported them to the Nazis, once they were arrested Soros would rob their homes and take their valuables. I don't know if that is true but I have seen some footage on YouTube pointing to this taking place. This is starting to sound like the NEW WORLD ORDER.

Many people were accused of being 'conspiracy theorists' about a lot of this that does not add up, but what I have discovered is that most of the so-called conspiracy theories have actually come true. As suddenly as George Floyd was all over the television screens night after night along with the rioting and mayhem stuffed down our throats, it just as suddenly stopped. No longer here in Australia was it being shown, no latest updates of what was going on in America, nothing, it just stopped overnight.

Facebook, YouTube and Twitter began censoring and removing, groups, posts and videos. All of a sudden there was no news about the riots and it went quiet to the point that I don't even try to find information about it now. Last week though, beginning of August 2020, I came across an article that the four Officers accused of Floyd's murder were found 'not guilty', apparently not long before the incident took place George had taken some drugs and it was now thought he was already dying from the amount he had taken, I don't know how true that is, maybe fake news, I am not sure.

In the meantime, the power of MSM continues flexing their almighty muscles. Who owns the media? It is thought whoever owns the media owns the world. This is, in fact, true because the majority believe everything they see or hear from MSM. Myself included at one time.

Along with all of the above taking place, Donald Trump still continued his daily Briefings at the White House and daily called out the MSM for reporting 'fake news'. He did not bat an eyelid about bringing them undone, exposing them for what they are. Trump continues to use Twitter and Facebook to put out a daily message so it is not construed into something it is not.

Meanwhile, here in Australia we still put up with the MSM and the narrative they want us to follow, we have no Prime Minister or Premiers calling the MSM out over here, they are in fact, deliberately using the MSM here to spread their propaganda and fear.

Linda M Noon

Chapter Nine: The Australian Narrative

Nothing Better Than Listening To A Lie When You Already Know The Truth - picturequotes.com

During this year of 2020, especially around April, May and June, the narrative on Covid-19 was basically panic, everywhere you looked it was Covid-19 morning, noon and night. I went along with it at first because I knew no better, but as I began to see and feel things were not right, I soon changed my mind about it all. Don't get me wrong, yes, there is a virus going around the world and it is killing people, mainly the elderly and immune-compromised as I mentioned earlier and it is terribly sad.

I went through days of fear and despair, totally sad inside. I had my year planned out and I thought I would be doing this, that and the other just like everyone else. My main concern was for my sons and especially my grandchildren who are very young and not even begun to have a life. The whole economy began to shut down, no more going out, no more parks or school for the kids. People losing their incomes and businesses. I never thought it would last this long. I don't think many of us did.

MSM were telling us how to wash our hands and disinfect everything. What I never understood is why do we need to use so many anti-bacterial products when this is a 'virus', doesn't 'anti-bacterial' kill bacteria and not viruses? Isn't it true that Anti-biotics don't work on viruses? We were being told that the Virus cannot live above 37 or 38 degrees Celsius, sunlight kills it. It lives up your nose and at the back of your throat.

People were being tested with test kits from China that were faulty and gave incorrect results. This was proven by an African President who sent a test from a pawpaw fruit, car engine oil and a goat. All came back positive for the Covid-19. How could this be? Those videos surfaced all over the place and were swiftly removed. Groups were forming on Social platforms asking the same questions as I was. Those groups were being removed, and censorship was rife on all platforms.

Doctors were coming forward with truths of their own that were quickly taken down. We were shown thousands of people dying and mass graves being dug around the world for all those who had died from this virus, we saw footage of overcrowded ICU wards in hospitals around the world, we saw people with some bubble looking bags over their heads in ventilators. We were told that hundreds of Chinese people were throwing their beloved pets off balcony's because they were told that their pet carried the virus. We were told two tigers in a zoo had contracted Covid-19 from their handlers and it went on and on. It was absolutely ridiculous!

Something had begun to change though, nurses and doctors were coming forward with their own stories that did not match up to what we were being told on MSM, they never came forward here in Australia though, mainly in America. The nurses were saying they are killing people, doctors were telling us to take 1000mg of Vitamin C, Zinc, Vitamin D and Tonic water as it contains Quinine. Also the anti-malaria drug known as Hydroxychloroquine, here in Australia it is known as Plaquenil which includes Quinine. These Doctors were removed from these platforms and we were told the reason why was because they were spreading 'false information'.

Suddenly all over Facebook each account was censored by 'Fact Checkers', if you posted anything that went against the MSM it was taken down and a message sat in its place saying you have shared false information. One group I was in on Facebook was taken down with no warning and it had 66,000 members. So you have no choice other than to start questioning things. This has nothing to do with conspiracies theories. Why are the public and Medical Professionals being censored? What happened to freedom of speech?

Trump was on our TV every day with this little Health Expert whom Trump at first was listening to, Dr Fauci. Australia was following America's and the UK's lead in this fight even though they denied they were, you could guarantee two days after America or the UK announced something Australia followed suit.

Dr Fauci is closely connected to Bill Gates and his Foundation are the biggest financial sponsors to the WHO, their agenda is to get all vaccinated with a vaccine that is going to be rushed through and Fauci said many years ago you cannot rush a vaccine until it has been vigorously tested but this year he said it must be pushed through and we can test it later. This same Dr Fauci in 2005 said worked wonders on the Covid and Coronavirus but this year said it is a dangerous drug and should not be used even though Donald Trump came out and openly shared months ago that he was taking it.

All of a sudden there has been a ban on Hydroxychloroquine. Any doctor here in Australia caught prescribing it will be fined $13,000 and may lose their license to practice. A huge businessman in Australia, Clive Palmer, bought 33 million bottles of it earlier in the year before it was banned and he gave them to our Government, his hope was that every person in Australia would get some.

Hydroxychloroquine has been used for years especially during the War in India to fight Malaria and was given to the soldiers in a glass of Tonic because it was so bitter, it still remains in the tonic to this day but in smaller amounts. So another WHY? Why is it banned if it works especially in the early stages of Covid-19, I have read if taken early enough along with Zinc it can knock out the virus within 24 hours. It has been banned here in Australia until October, why? WHY? Maybe because October there are elections?

Most of last year, 2019, I was looking for work although I did not find any, and into this year, 2020, I continued to look. Just before the Stage 1 restriction in March, I had a job interview at a family run business doing Administration. I was very confident about it too, only to receive an email the very next day telling me that due to the Covid-19 restrictions the position had been placed on hold. Things got worse for unemployment from then on, there are now 7.4% unemployed.

I can't for the life of me understand why the elderly and immune-compromised were not protected more than us healthy ones, nor why we cannot go about our usual business to keep the country running as our death rate is very low considering, and the recovery rate is very high at 99%. More and more questions surface every single day.

Many people had decided to visit hospitals that were claiming to be inundated with patients around Victoria and filming it, then posting their findings on Facebook with hardly any patients at all. Many MSM were showing hospitals around the world inundated with patients and then not long afterwards we were being shown that the same clips for Italy were shown in Australia and upon zooming in and watching the video, it was exposed that the patients in the beds were rubber dummies. People were beginning to wake up and call it a '*Plan*demic' which made me more curious to investigate.

I watched Dr Shiva, Dr Buttar, Vernon Coleman, David Icke and a guy named Harry Vox on YouTube, most of their videos were taken down. Harry Vox was talking back in 2014 about what is happening now, in 2020. He had a printed scenario that WHO had developed specifically for a Pandemic and the steps they used are exactly to a T what is happening right now around the world. People are claiming it is to usher in a New World Order where we will all be controlled.

I follow Peter Little, a lawyer who is trying to expose the Government for their tyranny and Draconian ways. They took his license from him and last week he lost his home and was sleeping in his car, someone started a go fund me page for him because he has done so much for many over the years pro bono and I now believe he has found a place on a campsite. Peter is not a young man either.

We are now, at time of writing this, in Stage 4 Restrictions for 6 weeks which is supposed to end on the 13th September, to be reviewed. What this means for us in Victoria is:

- Masks mandatory or receive a $1,652 fine.

- One person per household to go out for shopping once a day. (How do you control that?)

- 1 hour exercise once a day. (Like a prisoner in solitary in jail)

- Curfew 8pm-5am. (Why? Is the virus more deadly between those hours?)

- No visitors to your home or vice versa. (Isolation causes depression)

- There is a 5 kilometer radius that we are not allowed to go outside of. (Caged in)

- Police and POS have extra powers. (Unconstitutional)

- ADF have been brought in. (Why? People are being very, very compliant)

- Permit required to go to work even outside of the curfew hours. (Nazi Germany)

- Complete Border closure. (Melbourne is like being in East Berlin during the war and after the Wall went up)

Even if you know your rights at this time, we no longer have any because we were declared a State of Disaster and the Health Organization Laws outweigh them because the laws now say it is for the Health and Wellbeing of the Public.

There has never been a curfew in Australia not even during the War. Every day we hear on the TV the 'New Covid Norm'. This is not normal! Not to mention that there is even now a call for anyone going against the MSM and Government to be fined for being a Conspiracy Theorist. So if you question what is going on you are apparently a Conspiracy Theorist.

While all of this has been going on there have been major road works happening during the curfew hours not to mention many flights coming into Tullamarine Airport throughout the night from China yet there is supposed to be a flight ban. I saw the activities on the Traffic Radar Apps and the Flight Apps. I don't think anyone has to be a Conspiracy Theorist to ask what is going on or why. My gut has been telling me all along. People ask including myself, "If this virus is so contagious where are the Bio-hazard bins for all of the used masks?"

I follow their rules but it does not mean I do not ask questions like most Sleeping Beauties who may prefer to remain asleep. I feel it is also a test to see how far they can push us and how much control they have over us. Are our governments trying to incite riots here, to give them cause to arrest people?

The World is watching right now what is happening in Victoria. People are being abused in the streets for not wearing a mask even though they may have a medical reason not to, others are being arrested, even neighbours are calling hotlines to report their neighbours. Like dobbing in a Jew or homosexual during the war. It really is like being in Nazi Germany and I worry so much for my grandchildren. This is definitely overkill!

Donald Trump called out China in the beginning of this Pandemic calling it the 'China Virus' and our Prime Minister Scott Morrison backed him, then Japan backed us. China turned against us more than they turned on any other Country. China have called us 'chewing gum on the bottom of their shoe', and 'poor white trash of

Asia'. In the meantime Wuhan are up and running now enjoying rave, pool parties with thousands of attendees.

Yesterday, 13th August 2020 it was reported that our Premier Daniel Andrews would like to do more testing in rural Victoria even though there are no cases there at this present time. Again WHY? What is he looking for? What is he hoping to gain? Does he need more numbers? These are the questions that not only I ask but many other people ask.

In our MSM we have been told that singing Happy Birthday can spread the virus, speaking English is more likely to spread the virus and they are undecided whether to cancel day light savings this year because some expert has said it could potentially increase the risk of getting the virus. It is also reported that if out in public we are not allowed to sing or yell because this can spread the virus. Really!

In the UK there are posters inside the pubs letting customers know that if there is a football match on and it is televised then customers are not allowed to yell or shout if there is a goal kicked because no noise, no virus spread. Honestly, what is it all coming to? When the schools reopen in the UK they are thinking of closing the Pubs down again so the children can go to school. That just does not make any sense at all.

In the last week there have been four new cases in New Zealand all in the same family which cannot be traced to anywhere or anyone. New Zealand has swiftly gone back into Stage 3 restrictions only now there is a plan to remove people from their homes and place them into specially built quarantine facilities for fourteen days. What if you have a child who has the virus but no one else in the family does? How will that child cope with being removed from their family for fourteen days? What mental and emotional damage will that cause to a child? Will the child be safe from predators?

There are many questions to be asked about the severe implications and damage this could create, PTSD (Post Traumatic Stress Disorder) for a start. I am scratching my head trying to figure all of this out and still come up with answers. I feel like we are being led by some malfunctioning AI (Artificial Intelligence) morons and I liken the main population to the Stepford Wives, which is a movie about a town where all of the wives are robots and do everything asked of them without question. If this all makes sense to anyone, I would really like to know how they have managed to make sense of it all. Please enlighten me.

If I was a detective following a crime and I listened to the criminal and took their word for everything, I would not make a very good detective. Detectives go off hunches, intuition and the facts which they are faced with, they ask many questions. Hypothetically speaking this is what I and many others have been doing during the last few months. Critical thinkers have been labelled Conspiracy Theorists. The deeper one goes on the search for their truth the more questions arise. There is a burning feeling deep inside our souls that something is just not right!

I feel I have written what I have so far in the simplest way possible so as not to confuse whoever reads my words.

In the next chapter, I will go into a little more detail but be prepared for what I write because I lost a lot of sleep trying to digest what I found. It turned my stomach and made me feel physically sick at times. I had to take a break for a few days away from it all, vowing at times to not go back but once my conscious mind had assimilated what I knew, I was back on the trail.

Everything I have written can be researched via YouTube and other platforms and I strongly encourage you to do so, you have a right to know and maybe it is your duty to know, so maybe we are able to help others. It is not for me to provide everything for you, it is for me to try to Awaken the Lotus within you. You know, that DEEP INNER KNOWING. I ended up that far down the Rabbit hole I was almost up the Rabbit's arse.

Chapter Ten: The Deep State & Cabal

I Would Rather Be A Little Nobody, Than To Be An Evil Somebody
- Abraham Lincoln.

When things were not making sense to me early on during the Pandemic, I joined a few groups on Facebook to try to find answers. I saw a few comments here and there that lead me to do my own investigations rather than rely on someone else's words, and so it began. Sometimes I would make a comment and get attacked on Facebook if I did not agree with someone else.

I started to see a lot of arguments, people attacking people for not wearing masks as I said earlier, people calling others selfish for not wearing masks and so on. Bearing in mind that we had been told for over three months 'do not wear a mask as they do not work' and that advice was from the Government. Also wash your hands more, use Anti-bacterial, social distance. What people did not seem to understand is that a virus cannot be killed, Anti-bacterial hand sanitisers kill bacteria not viruses. Anti-biotics do not work on Viruses etc. Is it beginning to make sense?

I decided to move away from those groups and found others like Qanon, the information on there was what I was looking for even though, in the end, it got taken down from Facebook. I wonder why? I followed Qmap.pub on Google for the 'Q drops' and tried to make some sense of them. I met others in the groups who friended me and I them. Especially a young man in the UK called Matt, he was amazing and sent me plenty of links to get my teeth into and vice versa.

Then my friend Ted Exley in the UK let me know he was on the same page in a private message, which was great. Friends over here too started private messaging me. I found a little like-minded group in the friends I did not know shared the same basic instinct of, "Something is just not right here." Although with Qanon a lot of it is based on what

119

they share called Q drops, I have had trouble trying to find the evidance, so I look at it with an open mind because I want to believe it, and how exciting it is, but I still have no true evidence.

As my research expanded, I became more and more sceptical of the Government, CDC and the WHO, I subscribed to YouTube documentaries and received daily briefings about the topics I was researching. I was following David Icke until he was removed from all platforms and the good thing about David Icke is he had been saying stuff for years and years, well before I stumbled upon him. He had copped so much flak over the years because of his beliefs.

What was going on now was so close to his beliefs and it was very scary at first, but the more I listened the more it made sense. One day I was watching a video of Donald Trump and Donald himself said the 'Deep State' were out to get him and it was time he drained the swamp. Up until then, everything I had read about the Deep State was ridiculed as a conspiracy theory. When it came straight from Donald's mouth as far as I was concerned, it was no longer a conspiracy.

You may be wondering what is the Deep State? Well from what I have discovered it is the existence of Government Employees and others who secretly manipulate or control the Government without regard for the policies of Congress and the President of the United States. Dr Fauci is rumoured to be one of them and I feel the same going on here in Australia. They will do anything to take the Trump Government down BUT if you Google the Deep State it comes up that it is a Conspiracy Theory, thereby minimising its effects on the world and undermining what is really going on. Millions around the Globe do not believe the darkness going on and liken people like me to wearing a tinfoil hat.

President Trump knows he is not liked because he has done so much for his country unlike other World Leaders. Trump has kept all of his promises to his people, unlike ours who have not. The Deep State want him out and they have tried almost everything to achieve that without success so far. That is why many around the world are suspicious and waking up to this Covid-19 virus because it has come at a time that Donald Trump is running for his second term in Office.

The elections are to be held on 3rd November 2020 and most of us who are awakened pray that he succeeds because if he doesn't, and the Deep State get their way, the world will never go back to normal as we know it, we will be controlled and manipulated into mandatory vaccines, a cashless society, poverty and economic depression, which is already taking place. Right now we are living in a very scary, uncertain world.

The hidden enemies are all around us and the biggest enemy has been the MSM (Main Stream Media) with false data and the fixing of the numbers of deaths from Covid-19. Manipulation of the whole world. They are trying to herald in a New World Order, One World Government, one religion on a global scale. There has been a virus unleashed upon the world.

The masses are panic-stricken with fear. The suicide rate in Australia alone has more than doubled within the first four months of the virus, far more than we have had deaths from the virus. The majority have been male suicides, men with families and now children losing their dads, the children are another casualty of this virus.

The Cabal often referred to as the Illuminati, Deep State, Shadow Government or the Elite. Now being known for Pedophilia, Child Sex Trafficking, Media Manipulation and Ritual Sacrifices of stolen babies and children and the drinking of their blood, after they have been drugged, raped and tortured the adrenal glands releasing adrenaline into the blood and apparently, when it is drunk, it is supposed to contain the fountain of youth, Adrenochrome. A very sickening thought to ever comprehend, it took me a while to get my head around that one. I spent many sleepless nights because of this.

The people involved were supposed to have been Jefferey Epstein (he was jailed for sex trafficking and reportedly committed suicide in jail), Ghislaine Maxwell (currently in Jail awaiting trial for child sex trafficking and being the right hand man of Epstein), Hillary Clinton (due in Court on 9 September 2020 for many emails that we hope incriminates her and 52 people she has known have been killed), Barrack Obama, Prince Andrew, the Pope and many in Hollywood. Tom Hanks (took off to live in Greece and became a Greek citizen because they have no extradition laws), Will Farrell, Will Smith, Johnny Depp, Alec Baldwin, Beyonce, Oprah, Lady Gaga, Madonna, Ellen DeGeneres (currently being investigated for being a mean person on her show), Robert DeNiro and that is to only name but a few.

There is a list of names in Epstein flight log that has been circulating for some time, taking these people to his Private Island for these disgusting acts to have taken place. You can research that. Even though I cannot tell you if it is really true as I have no evidence other than YouTube and what others share on FB, but those are the rumors and names being shared around. I like to think the above Hollywood names are not like that or even involved, but because of such a crazy year 2020 anything is possible.

The Queen has also been implicated in the past, I think it was in the late '60s, of abducting some children, as they never returned from a picnic she took them on. Prince Andrew refuses to talk with the FBI about his connection to Epstein and the photos that surfaced of him with an underaged girl so that part is true and then Prince Harry left the Royal family to live in America with his wife Megan.

Hollywood is involved up their necks and the Hollywood actor Mel Gibson tried to warn the world about this over ten years ago, but he was labelled a 'nut case'. He did lose the plot for a while and now we know why.

Avicii, Chester Bennington, Anthony Bourdain & Chris Cornell all supposedly 'committed suicide' while working on a documentary called THE SILENT CHILDREN about widespread Pedophilia and Trafficking. Isaac Kappy came out with more claims about Steven Spielberg and died 13ᵗʰ May 2019, apparently another suicide. Rumour has it that Tom Hanks ordered his murder, and Corey Feldman has also tried to speak out.

It is reported that other Child Sex Trafficking rings have gone on for many, many years all around the world, with underground tunnels, most of the children do not have a birth certificate and so are not missed because no one really knows that they exist. There are also reports claiming that they are organ harvesting too from newborn babies. Hence while in lockdown there have been a few abortion laws passed that allow abortion right up until full term.

There have been children sold online shopping websites such as Wayfair, Amazon, Etsy and Ebay. Sold as furniture with a child's name for exuberant prices. Some of that has been confirmed by Tim Ballard, who rescues these children and has his own website called ourrescue.org and to me he is a real hero. There is a movement now circulating around Facebook called #saveourchildren. He has rescued thousands but there are still many thousands to be saved. All of these Elite Pedophile Rings use symbolism and codes and they are all over the world wide web, if you are a pedophile you would know where to look for them.

There is a story about Barrack Obama ordering $60,000 worth of 'Pizza' and 'Hotdogs' at 4am one time (Wiki Leaks). 'Pizza' being code for little girls. Obamagate; what is all that about? I don't want to get into this too deeply through this book, I am relying on people to do their own research because this still makes my stomach turn. I am only wishing to touch the tip of the iceberg, so to speak, in the hope that this will lead you to you own investigations, if you so choose and not relying on what I have written.

This is the Great Awakening and I have named this book The Awakening Of The Lotus for this very reason. I am throwing you crumbs in the hope you will awaken to the bigger picture of what is actually happening right now in the world.

Will our world ever return to being normal or will it deteriorate from here on in?

Yesterday, 16th August 2020, I read that in New Zealand they have built Quarantine camps, anyone returning to NZ will be placed in one for 14 days, if they refuse to be tested they will have to stay there a month. I also discovered that for the past few weeks, Bill Gates (the one who wants us all mandatorily vaccinated) has been in NZ with the Premier Jacinta Adern. I have read that if a family member contracts Covid-19 the government will have the power, without your approval, to remove your children and take them out of the home for 14 days.

Why, when children don't seem to catch it? What will they do to them? Will they be allowed back home? Or will they disappear and you be told they have died from Covid-19? How scary is that thought and what can we do about it if this does happen? How traumatic would that be for the children?

The more your read and discover the more it feels like a War and Nazi Germany. The measures that have been taken are too extreme for a virus that has a 99.7% recovery rate. As at 11th August 2020, there were according to the MSM, 21 Million infected worldwide, 760,000 Deaths and 13 Million recoveries. Nothing adds up. What happened to the other 7 Million?

Many believe that it is more likely connected to the role out of the 5G towers being activated all around the world that have created this illness within our bodies because of the high intensity of the Electro Magnetic Radiation, the first city in the world to be blanketed with 5G was Wuhan, the belief is that the body reacts like it has a virus every time there is a surge in new higher frequencies and it is not a virus entering our bodies at all, nor a Pandemic.

The reason the elderly are most affected is because their immune systems are not strong enough and the symptoms are so close to radiation poisoning. That is why I wear my Tesla Pendent, I have known about them for years and have had one for twenty years which I wear day and night, especially now.

~*~

My belief is this: Whether it is the manmade virus or 5G, or a bit of both, it is done to push a vaccine on the entire population of the world via Bill Gates, without correct and safe testing, AI artificial intelligence and cashless society. It has been timed to strike the world at this time and this year because of the American Elections coming up in November 2020. Agenda 21.

It has been aimed at America, Europe and the UK to cause sheer panic and the collapse of the World Economy to prevent Donald Trump from being voted back in. The Deep State see him as a huge threat and they are scared because he has drained the Swamp and he has saved many children from child sex trafficking. He created more employment and their economy was thriving again until the China Virus or 5G. He works tirelessly without pay.

I feel the reason why Australia has not been hit as hard as other countries in the world is because China owns most of Australia and they are not going to destroy what they have a vested interest in. It was probably a pure accident that Australia copped it, initially from the Ruby Princess. Not forgetting those Cruise Ships are loaded with 5G as well.

I feel that even our government are a part of the Deep State as they also protect Pedophiles especially in the Judicial system as well as a former Prime Ministers because from my research I found out a 99 year suppression order was signed off by Gary Crooke QC a former senior counsel assisting NSW Wood Royal Commission into Police corruption in the 1990's. Some say it was John Howard who signed off on it and some say it was Scott Morrison, but I am not too sure about that, I haven't found anything on them, unless that has also been removed.

Victoria and New Zealand are very close to China and have many deals with them and I feel Daniel Andrews is only a puppet and he is being told what to do by the Deep State. I feel they are testing to see how far Victorian's can be pushed and how much we will tolerate and so far, it has all gone in the government's favour.

I feel that if Donald Trump does not win the elections we will be stuffed as a race and totally controlled by the Rothschilds, Rockefellers, Soros, Bill Gates, the UN, and the WHO and whoever else is involved in the NEW WORLD ORDER.

Donald Trump has said that the Deep State don't like him and don't want him there and that AG 'Bill' Barr is investigating to find out who they are and they may be trialled for Treason.

- Quote: "It is time to Drain the Swamp of the Pedophiles and Child Sex Trafficking."

- Quote: "Osama Bin Laden had nothing to do with the 9/11 Towers."

- Quote: "Every day the MSM report fake news about me and I call them out on it."

- Quote: "There are some very rich men that do not like me and I may disappear for a while."

Recently Trump signed an executive order to protect children from going into care at all costs.

This link shows Trump's 289 accomplishments in just 20 months with every promise kept:

https://www.washingtonexaminer.com/washington-secrets/trumps-list-289-accomplishments-in-just-20-months-relentless-promise-keeping

If he was a liar, he would not have accomplished what he has done, until Covid-19 struck, and if America is made great again, so we all shall be. When Trump makes the statement "MY FELLOW AMERICANS THE STORM IS UPON US" that is when we will know it is all in perfect order and some heavy stuff is going down. It is said to look to Twitter for this message.

My awakening to Covid-19 is condensed into these pages because each day I discover something new and so I cannot possibly write it all in this book otherwise this book would not be about Awakening, it would be about the Covid-19 and that is not my intention for this book. I only ask that you trust your own instinct and your own inner knowing, trying to write about Covid-19 in a book is a mind boggling adventure. My mind and inner knowing understands it all but I cannot put it in into words. I don't even want to try.

You will know and your mind will assimilate it into your being for you but if you decide to investigate for yourself be prepared for a range of emotions and sleepless nights before it is assimilated. My advice would be don't try to explain it to anyone else unless they are on the same page because you will come across as a person wearing a tinfoil hat. Don't be afraid to plant a seed though, there may be one person waiting for a word that will contain immense power to wake them up. You know, just like the virus can infect one, then that one can infect three and so on, or so they say, well the same thing applies to a seed of truth.

I am not trying to convince you of anything, you have your own free will and your own INNATE INNER KNOWING.

In years to come, many will write their own experience of Covid-19 which will include all of the nitty-gritty, dates, times, events, facts and stats but that is not what I want to write about even though I could. Please research and discover for yourself, it is the only way you will find your *own* truth.

There is much Darkness in this world much more then we could ever comprehend, low life in high places, so to speak. It is not all rainbows and butterflies. The Darkness must embrace the Light and the Light must shine brightly onto the Darkness for humanity to survive. We need to be led from the darkness and into the light.

That is what I feel is happening, the Light is beginning to shine and expose the Darkness in such a way that the Darkness can no longer hide. Love and protect our children for they are the way of the future, love and protect yourself and all other sentient beings and life. Like the Lotus that grows out of the mud into a beautiful flower.

Chapter Eleven: Freedom Day

Freedom Is Not Voluntarily Given By The Oppressor,
It Must Be Demanded By The Oppressed.
Freedom Quote Via Gecko & Fly

On 9th August 2020, Victoria's State of Emergency was extended for another six weeks taking up to 13 September 2020, this meant Stage 4 restrictions were to remain in place, much to public dismay and outcry. Our Premier, Danial Andrews, was on some kind of one-man power trip aimed at all of Victoria, demanding everyone get tested for Covid-19, mandatory face masks and failure to wear one carried a $200 fine. Permits needed to travel to work at any time, a curfew between the hours of 8pm-5am, only one person per household to go out shopping, rations, one hour of exercise and a 5km radius of travel.

All businesses closed, all schools closed. Only four reasons to leave your home, weddings not allowed, churches closed and only ten people at a funeral. People to work from home where they could. Drones flying overhead in the suburbs and along the coastal shores to make sure people are not on the beaches. Military presence, extreme Police powers which allows them to enter your home without a warrant and remove children or remove the tenants, destroy or take anything they want to away from us that 'they feel is necessary'. My mind boggles at the question, "Why?" It is so unnecessary.

As the long days passed by, I became alerted to a group on Facebook who were organising a protest in the Melbourne CBD sometime in September, although there was no date given at the time, but we were told to look out for a smiley face to appear. Finally, the smiley face appeared, the protest was for Freedom Day, 5th September 2020 at 12pm, place to be arranged. A peaceful gathering for Freedom, to take our freedoms back, no more lockdowns.

Each day I checked the numbers of the growing support for this day and as it stood at time of writing this section, 26ᵗʰ August 2020, there were 14,000 planning to attend. Not only that, it was going to be Australia wide, in every single state in support for us in Victoria. I decided that I wanted to take part in this for my grandchildren and their future, this can no longer go on, ruining people's lives and livelihoods.

I felt I have to take part, because if I sit and do nothing I can no longer complain about the tyranny of our dictator Danial Andrews, breaking every law and removing our constitutional rights. The elderly and the sick need to be protected, and I feel the rest of us must get on with our lives and reopen the economy. Our children and grandchildren are going to be paying for this for generations to come.

We want our borders opened and we do not consent to getting a mandatory unsafe, rushed vaccine, which contain enough toxic chemicals to kill a horse. Did you know that by the time a child is 18 years old, from birth they will have received up to 72 vaccines in their lives? Why? The ingredients are not safe, I will list but a few: Phenoxyethanol (insecticide), aluminium (neurotoxin), fetal bovine serum (aborted calves blood), formaldehyde (carcinogen, embalming agent), gelatin (ground up animal carcasses), human albumin (human blood), MRC-5 cells (*aborted human babies*), potassium chloride (used in lethal injection to stop the heart and shut down breathing), urea (metabolic waste from human urine) and much, much more, the list goes on and on.

Would you like to inject all of that on top of whatever else, to stop this virus, when they haven't even got a vaccine that works for the common cold or flu? The flu vaccine only covers four strains, but there are over 150 strains of flu. Why all of these toxic ingredients? If they want us to be healthy, by all means create a vaccine, but create a safe one without all of the other crap.

Most Victorians are no longer happy to sit back and allow Dan to dictate to us. Even though we were not allowed out of our 5km travel zone, I was still going to attend, $1642 fine or no fine, I felt I must go.

24th August 2020, Danial Andrews appeared for his daily briefing on the TV and we were all told that he was extending the state of emergency for another 12 months into September 2021. This has infuriated the public even more, as well as Parliament and local MP's. This time there is far more anger and uproar than before. The people of Victoria have had enough.

Suicide rates and family Murder/Suicides are at an all-time high. The majority are suffering for the minority, as sad as it is for the elderly to be the ones dying, and dying alone without family around them. The amount of deaths from Covid-19 are around 400 as it stands after six months of the 'deadly killer virus', the Premier's reactions are overkill and it feels like we are in a war zone. Even though the numbers have dropped to around one hundred, fortunately the people are not taking this lying down this time around, there have been letters and emails sent far and wide to the Government to stop this lunatic Danial Andrews.

The Chief Medical Officer, Brett Sutton, also said on Sunday 23rd August 2020, "Numbers are low and will not climb again," and I quote him, "Not on my watch." That statement jumped straight out at me which lead me to think, "How can he possibly say that, like he has some control over the virus or does he know it is all inflated and embellished in the first place?" If that is to be the case, then why would they worry about a protest, if the numbers will not climb again? After all, CMO Brett Sutton said so.

Already MSM have jumped onto the bandwagon, calling the organisers of the Freedom Day March a dangerous cult, the MSM are reporting the 14,000 people attending the march and another 13,000 interested, 'believe the virus is a hoax'. Not one person going thinks the virus is a hoax, they think like I am thinking, the low figures do not add up to justify such a severe lockdown.

On 26th August 2020, Facebook deleted the group organising the protest with over 14,000 attendees. Why? What are they so afraid of? One of the organisers changed his profile picture with the place and time, 5th September 2020 at the Shrine of Remembrance at 11am.

27th August 2020, the media were reporting Danial Andrews had come to a compromise and will extend the State of Emergency to 6 months instead of 12 months.

If he is successful this is what he wants: The Public Health & Wellbeing Act: 2008 definition changed under section 3 to add a section 3.4 sub act. "Serious Covid-19 Public Risk". Even when the rate is low or no Covid-19 rates have been seen for some time, it allows the State of Emergency to remain in place to enable enforcement and extension of Concentrated Executive Powers of the lockdown laws.

This is highly dangerous for Daniel Andrews to have this amount of power along with the Chief Medical Officer, Brett Sutton. At this stage, they could relax the restrictions, but what the above means, is they can revert back to the above, at any time they choose, for whatever reason they choose, in the name of Public Health & Wellbeing, even though the data collected for the Covid-19 does not warrant such extreme measures.

This terrifies me more than any virus. I am scared for my grandchildren and their future. At this stage I hope, all of the emails to the government carry some weight from the public, to not allow Danial Andrews to succeed on his mission to totally obliterate the State of Victoria and the Victorians' way of life pre Covid-19.

On some sort of positive note though, our Prime Minister, Scott Morrison has voiced his opinion about Danial Andrews' 'Road Belt Contract', signed with Beijing, against the advice of our Prime Minister in the past. Scott Morrison has threatened to rip the contract up, for fear it may not be in the best interest of the Australian People. We will have to wait and see if that happens.

While Sheila and I were waiting for the 5ᵗʰ September, I decided to get us a T-shirt each made from Vistaprint, with the smiley face on it, the date, and 'I do not consent' slogans on the backside of the T-shirt. In between all of that the date was the 13ᵗʰ September, then it changed to the 5ᵗʰ September, there was much confusion about it all. Finally, we were reassured it was the 5ᵗʰ September 2020 at the Shrine of Remembrance in Melbourne CBD.

We set about planning our route into the CBD and to arrive there without detection from the Police because there had been threats made by the Police Commissioner about arrests and 'our feet would not touch the ground', if anyone attended. Two nights before the protests there was a message going around Facebook letting people know that the march had been postponed because of the arrests taking place of the organisers for 'Incitement'. It became a bit of a shambles, people were up in arms about the confusion, many said they were still going.

Sheila and I decided we were still going and sticking to our plan. We decided to leave our phones at home, and bought a cheap one for the day, only in case we got separated at any point. We drove the back-way into North Melbourne, via Point Cook, Altona, through Footscray and up Dynon Road and parked outside the Lort Smith's Lost Dogs Home, we planned to catch two trams to the Shrine, all without being stopped by the Police. The week before we were practising mentally, placing a large mirrored egg-shape around us, to reflect any attention away for us and become invisible to the Police.

We were both nervous and excited at the same time, because we knew we were taking a risk of receiving many fines and even arrest, and possibly getting turned back, but the need to do it for our children and grandchildren and the future was far greater. Our t-shirts arrived a few days before the event, we were so happy with them.

The morning of the 5th September arrived and up I got and went off to Sheila's, we had a backpack each with lunch and water to drink. We had also planned that if we were stopped in the CBD that we only lived 5km away in Richmond, we had an address, but we also took no ID with us.

9am, off we set and each suburb we went through we felt excited to be getting closer and closer to our destination. Finally we arrived at Villier Street, North Melbourne, but right where we were to get on a tram there was a huge Police barricade, the Police were stopping everyone. We drove around the block and found a back street to park in.

Because the Police were set up right where we were going to board a Tram we decided not to get on the Tram and began walking into the CBD. After getting lost a few times and going around in circles we found ourselves slap bang in the middle of the CBD, but we had to get over to the other side.

There was a huge Police presence, they were on foot and in groups of five, each time we turned a corner there they were, and each time I said to Sheila, "We are invisible, in our mirrored egg." Without fail the Police continued walking by us and stopping others behind us or to the left of us. It was rather comical, I said, "Oh! If anyone could hear us, they would think we were mad." We had a few giggles but the walk seemed never ending.

Finally we saw Flinders Street Station up ahead along with another large group of Police, we were almost at our destination and really did not want to be stopped, as we both knew we had broken every rule except curfew. Like we were really invisible the Police did not even look at us and we kept on going towards the Shrine. This all meant we had actually walked right through the thick of it to get there with the amount of Police we past on the way, unbelievable we did not get stopped once, and we were wearing a face covering with a skeleton face on them.

Arriving at the Shrine, there was a huge Police presence and we saw the crowd in the distance and kept walking towards them, finding ourselves right in the middle of it. What an amazing feeling to have made it and the crowd were so peaceful, we sang and chanted FREEDOM!

There were a row of officers all the way around the Shrine and behind them on the top of the steps were twelve officers on horseback, what an amazing sight, the Police had begun to circle us but not aggressively, until someone in the crowd yelled out, "March." We all began to march towards Albert Park Lake, it was then I saw the amount of peaceful protestors, there must have been 1,500 to 2,000. There should have been a lot more, but because of the stuff-ups about the dates and postponements, whoever could get there, did so.

As we marched to the Lake, traffic were tooting their horns in support, people in their apartments came onto their balconies, filming and waving, it was extremely peaceful and we were proud we made it there, to be a part of it and the history in the making. There were choppers following us and also an army chopper, we marched around the path of the lake for quite some time, the weather was beautiful, Sheila and I even reminisced about how we used to go to the Lake as children to go rowing.

We had roughly been marching for around two hours, when the group decided to make their way back to the Shrine, we gathered in the street to listen to what the next plan was to be, it was at that point I got an uneasy feeling, I turned to Sheila and said, "I think we should leave it here for us, I have a bad feeling it is going to turn nasty." The group had decided to go back to the Lake, we decided not to follow, at that point I saw a roadblock ahead, the Police on horses coming down the road and four mounted Police across the road. We were near a Tram stop so we decided to act like we were waiting for a tram.

Then it went a bit nuts, there were 28 black Police cars, 2 black lock-up vans and one white lock up van and they came driving like madmen down the tram tracks, I do not know why they did that, there was no traffic on the road at all because they had blocked it off. Sirens were blazing, 'overkill' is how I will describe it. That was when the crowd dispersed, because they knew the Police were now turning nasty, after letting us go for two hours, they must have received orders from the Commissioner. A smallish group ran towards the lake, maybe 60 to 80 and the Police went after them, away from the street.

What was unbelievable, the Police came out in riot gear, WHY? There was no riot, there was only peace. They began jumping on people, 5 to 1, while the whole time, it was being filmed from the news helicopter above. They arrested a few, and the rest they made sit on the grass, while the tough riot police encircled them, like Custer's last stand, rather embarrassing and so much overkill. It was the Police who started the heavy-handed stuff, *not the protestors*.

Sheila and I had begun walking back towards Flinders Street, a walk that went on and on, with tired, sore feet, hips and legs, for us old Grannies, we felt a great feeling of accomplishment, we achieved what we set out to do, and did not get stopped once. By the time we were almost at Flinders Street we no longer cared if we got stopped, we were too tired. We decided when we arrive there, we will jump into a taxi, because our old legs could not face the rest of the walk back into North Melbourne to find the car, plus by this time, we were both walking like we had two wooden legs.

We arrived at Flinders Street and climbed into a taxi, what a great feeling that was. Finally arriving at where we parked the car, we climbed inside and set off home, still not caring if we got stopped, we went home on the freeway and it was a clear, smooth drive all the way back home. I was glad I listened to my feeling of things turning bad, I don't think I would have liked to be pushed on the ground.

Later that day waiting for the 6pm news to come on, so that we may see what 'fake news' they were going to use, and we were definitely not disappointed with that. The MSM story, was there were only about 80 to 100 people who turned up to protest. Lie! The aerial footage captured the small handful of protestors who had run back to the lake, how embarrassing for the news.

Five Riot Police arrested an elderly male, they were walking him away, when a riot Police Officer walked up to him and sprayed him in the face with pepper spray. WHY? They already had him in cuffs, he was not resisting. Two old ladies sitting on a bench were next, Police snatching a phone out of her hands.

The best thing to happen on the 5th is all the other states in Australia had very successful protests in support for us here in Victoria, it was amazing and very humbling to see, we thank each and every one of them, not only them but Canada, Sweden and London. The world is with us, standing up for Freedom.

Sunday 6th September, waiting for Daniel Andrews to give his speech on his 'Road Map Out of Restrictions', what a huge disappointment that was. As of 11.59pm Sunday 13th September, curfew will start at 9pm instead of 8pm, one person can visit one other person who lives alone, parks will open, and the big one... we can now have 2 hours outside to exercise instead of 1 hour, this will be for an extra 2 weeks after the 13th September 2020. Still no businesses to open, all this dragging on well into October and November. For 600 deaths so far, Victoria has endured the longest lockdowns worldwide.

Monday 7th September 2020, I have seen on many platforms that protests are really going to begin here in Victoria and Australia each weekend, I really hope there is a much, much bigger crowd, as it should have been on the 5th in the first place. The world will be protesting every weekend, I believe the people are awake to all of this now, our participation on the 5th was just to crack the egg.

Australia has been the slowest to react, to this tyranny and dictatorship, better late than never. One good thing happened today, Scott Morrison, has made it clear to Daniel Andrews that he is not happy with his Road Map Out of Restrictions, and has said, "This should have been the worst-case scenario." Daniel's arrogant reply was, "No, it's not."

We achieved what we set out to achieve. I am in the now, with the fear of the future, but without the past, and what our ancestors fought for, there would be no now, and without now, there will be no future. As they say, "time waits for no man," what we do now, will shape the future of our forthcoming generations. Dictatorship does not happen overnight, it is something that creeps in slowly, with silent consent and complacency. Trust your inner guidance, when something does not feel right, it is usually because it isn't.

We are not meant to be under 'house arrest', curfew, mandatory masks, rations, permits to work, mandatory vaccines, closed economies, closed schools, no work, increased suicides, increased domestic violence, increased childhood sexual abuse for being stuck at home with a perpetrator with no escape, and 5km radius zones or cages, kept away from family, friends the elderly and dying.

For what? A virus with a 99% survival rate, a virus that has the same symptoms of the flu and the exact same complications for the elderly and immune-compromised of a flu. At this moment in time, August 2020, there are in Australia 1,000 less deaths of the elderly this year, than last year, when we had no Covid-19, go figure. While Wuhan is now enjoying thousands of people raving at pool parties.

There are many who love Daniel Andrews and believe he is doing a great job, but he was the one who stuffed everything up, with the hotel quarantines and lies about the ADF, not to mention the branch staking he still has to face. I have been attacked on my own social media, if I go against the mainstream, and only last night, 6/8/2020, I came up with a new word for those people and I love it. I now refer to them as the DANDROIDS. I have been called selfish and, "It's people like you" etc. I have not broken any laws, all the way through this, until the 5th September, even then I don't think I broke any justified laws by standing up for my constitutional rights.

I tell you, what I find selfish, the people who sit at home listening to the lies and believing them, without doing any research, without looking into anything, yet attack someone who does. I find it selfish that right at the start of this, the elderly and vulnerable were not protected, and they still are not. If anyone thinks that they are being protected because they are in lockdown, away from their families and visitors, where they are losing the hope to live and dying alone, you are mistaken.

I find it selfish for the aged care system to employ three casuals to work across three different age care homes, with the high potential to cross-contaminate. I find it selfish that no one is thinking about the ones who are committing suicide, because they have lost everything they have worked for, including their homes and no-one is talking about it. I find it selfish that child sexual abuse in the home has multiplied, because the schools are closed and there is no escape for the young ones, and no one is talking about it.

I find it selfish that many think the young are not scared, and that they too are selfish. I think it is selfish for everyone to be scared of a virus where there is a 99% recovery. I find it selfish that most people do not have enough confidence in their own immune systems, because they know they have abused their bodies with all sorts of rubbish and bad diets.

I think it is selfish to expect the majority to lose everything in the fight to save the minority, we are being told and forced, not asked, to sacrifice our lives for the minority when there have been only 661 deaths, and even those numbers are fudged. I think it is selfish for all other surgeries and treatments to have been cancelled, causing far more deaths than Covid-19 has caused.

I think it is selfish that most are sitting waiting, for an unsafe vaccine, with the potential to kill you, and expect everyone to have the vaccine too, against their wishes. You won't need to worry about catching Covid-19 from an unvaccinated person, will you? Because you will be safe from it! Won't you?

These are my thoughts and opinions, many have different opinions, but that should not make us hate one another, or turn against one another. We need to respect one another. This is how I awakened, and I am not alone, the whole world is awakening, all relatively at the same time, it is not a conspiracy when millions upon millions are marching for truth and freedom, collectively all over planet Earth. It is absolutely amazing.

I will observe with bated breath, that which unfolds around us as a collective worldwide consciousness, and I live in great hope that the light will prevail, very soon, for all to live in harmony, peace and with bright futures ahead.

THE AWAKENING OF THE LOTUS
(Light Of The Universal Source/Sun/Son)

Epilogue/Conclusion

The key points to this book are to follow what you feel to be true for you. Trust your instinct and intuition.

Keep a dream diary and write whatever you wake up with, usually the most profound message or image in a dream means the most.

Meditation is a great way to tap into your inner power and knowings. Meditation means to listen, as hard as it may be at first try to still your mind from thought even if you start with only 5 minutes a day and expand on that.

The hidden power is within your mind and the mind never ever stops, when you are awake it thinks all day, consciously and sub-consciously, while you are sleeping it dreams and processes the events of the day. So to be able to still the mind while you are awake and conscious is powerful. The stilling of the mind is your key into the higher dimensions and it comes naturally with practice. It is not supernatural, it is natural.

Stay fit and healthy, eat clean foods, get sunlight and plenty of sleep. Stock up on 1000mg of Vitamin C a day, with Zinc and a glass of Tonic Water which contains Quinine.

I hope some of my stories help you to reconnect to a part of you that you may have neglected as the time has gone by and they trigger some memory of your own innate gifts.

I have thrown in many seeds throughout the pages of this book in the hope you begin to question and becoming more aware of what is going on within you and your surroundings.

At the very least I hope it has entertained and given you food for thought.

There is no end at this point, this is really just the beginning even though this pandemic has been many years in the planning, I am sure when it is written into World History it will contain many lies and fabricated material. Whether you like Trump or not, don't worry about that, just be open-minded to his achievements and promises kept for his country. This book is not about Politics.

I am Awakened now, and I cannot *unawaken* from it, nor do I wish to. I can only watch as it all unfolds, and assimilate it into my Awakened-ness.

Trust your intuition at all times, listen to your dreams,
be peaceful and be love.

Bibliography

Sources of information:

Alice Down The Rabbit Hole ~ YouTube

Alan Jones ~ Sky News

AG Bill Barr ~ YouTube ~ Trumps Attorney General

Donald Trump ~ YouTube, Facebook and Twitter

Dr Battar ~ FB & YouTube

Dr Shiva ~ FB & YouTube

David Icke ~ YouTube

Fanos Panayides ~ Facebook

Harry Vox ~ YouTube

ITNJ Chief Counsel Robert David Steele ~ YouTube (inquiry into child sex trafficking)

Nesara/Gesara (Check this one out!)

Operation Underground Railroad ~ YouTube & Internet

Tim Ballard www.ourrescue.org / YouTube/ #saveourchildren

Vernon Coleman ~ YouTube

Qanon ~ YouTube ~ WWG1WGA (where we go one we go all)

Qmap.pub Internet

Videos to watch:

The Cabal ~ especially Ep 5, Out of Shadows and Pizzagate

Q - The Plan To Save The World

Avicii ~ A Better Day (song)

Mel Gibson ~ Why he left Hollywood.

Acknowledgments

Thank you to my Editor & Publisher Michael Young of www.AvaOrionMedia.com who inspired me to write. Who I class as a dear friend as well.

Ted Exley a longtime friend in the UK for his inspiration to kick start me into writing this book.

Sheila Warne a lifelong friend from 1973 who is mentioned throughout and with whom I shared many adventures and has always been a part of my brain matter only she was the grey bit. That is a personal joke between us.

My sons for being in my life and being a huge part of my Journeys.

My sister Tracey, brother Mick and Dad for the memories that I was able to include in these pages.

Thank you to the Veever's Family for my early childhood memories in Salford and the only place that I ever thought existed in my world.

To Lauren & Master Thang and the many friends I have known throughout my life including the ones I now share my time with when not in lock down.

Jannelle Jordon, Michael Young, Christine Scott and my Daughter-In-Law Stef.

To the friends and like-minded community on Facebook. Particularly Rose Farrugia, Matt Reyyq and Timothy Archer.

Thank you also to the ones who may not share my truths but in a way contributed to my words unknowingly.

To every person I have interacted with, throughout my life, that helped to inspire my words.

Thank you to my Grandchildren for bringing me much love, joy and the strength to fight for you, your future and your freedom and for the freedom of all children. Never before have I had a truer cause, than to fight for your rights, in every sense of the word. I want my Grandchildren to know, I did not remain silent!

About the Author

Linda M Noon

- 2012 Certificate III in Government

- 2002-Pres Clinical Hypnotherapist.Dip.Clin.Hyp

- 1999-2002 Certificates Buddhist Philosophy & Meditation

- 1999 Meditation Teacher

- 1998 Reiki Master/ Teacher

- 1994 UK Fitness & Nutrition Diploma

Lives in Werribee, Victoria Australia

https://Chambersoflight.com

Email: awakeningofthelotus@outlook.com

Enjoys Art, Crafts & writing Poetry as well as spending time with my Family and Friends.

Love my dog Choco who never judges me.

The great outdoors and Road Trips.

A Love of helping others.

Made in the USA
Columbia, SC
26 October 2020